LYLE E. SCHALLER

REFLECTIONS OF A CONTRARIAN

SECOND THOUGHTS ON THE PARISH MINISTRY

ABINGDON PRESS

Nashville

Reflections of a Contrarian
Second Thoughts on the Parish Ministry

Copyright © 1989 by Abingdon Press

This book is printed on acid-free paper.

Library of Congress Cataloging-in-Publication Data

SCHALLER, LYLE E.
    Reflections of a contrarian.
ISBN 0-687-35888-4 (alk. paper)
    1. Pastoral theology.   2. Theology,
Practical.   I. Title.
BV4011.S335   1989   253   88-7871

Manufactured by the Parthenon Press at Nashville, Tennessee,
United States of America

Warren Hartman

Contents

Introduction

When I was a pastor in Wisconsin in the 1950s, I assumed that when someone died, the number-one client at that funeral service would be the grieving survivors. It disturbed me when the wife of the thirty-five-year-old son would take me aside the day before that memorial service and plead, "Reverend, please keep it short." I perceived that occasion as both an opportunity and a challenge to speak to that family, as well as to the assembled friends and kinfolk, on the Christian view of death.

Many years later I discovered the real world. I learned that at next Tuesday's memorial service, the number-one audience for what the preacher has to say about the Christian view of death probably will not be the immediate family of the deceased. The number-one client may be the cousin of the deceased who was widowed eight months ago. Or that most responsive listener may be a neighbor of the deceased who is still hurt, angry, and baffled over the death of his seventeen-year-old son in an automobile accident two years ago. Or the person who will be most affected by that message may be the fifty-nine-year-old man who, for the first time in his life, is now wrestling with his own mortality.

Likewise the congregations I served gathered for the corporate worship of God on Sunday morning. While we worshiped together on other occasions during the course of the year, Sunday morning was the regularly appointed time to come together to worship God, to sing His praises, to offer our prayers of thanksgiving and intercession, to observe the sacraments of baptism and Holy Communion, to listen to the Word, and to celebrate the resurrection of our Lord and Savior. No one questioned that choice of Sunday morning as the appropriate time for this congregation to come together for the corporate worship of God.

Subsequently, as I became better acquainted with the Seventh Day Baptists, the Seventh-Day Adventists, and other Christian traditions, I began to understand the range of biblical arguments that can be mustered in support of identifying the seventh day, not the first day of the week, as the Sabbath.

The point of these two illustrations is the central thesis of this book. What you believe influences what you do. If you are convinced the immediate family is the number-one audience for that funeral sermon, you will follow one approach in preparing it. If you are convinced you cannot be sure who will be most profoundly influenced by that message, and it may be a complete stranger, you will follow a different route in preparing it.

Likewise, if you believe that Christians should follow the example of Christ and the Apostles in choosing a day to be set aside for the worship of God, or if you are convinced the definitive issue in the struggle between God and the Beast is the choice of the day to be called the Sabbath or if you believe in the primacy of the Fourth Commandment, you will choose the seventh day as the Sabbath.

If, however, you believe the resurrection of Jesus is the key in choosing that special day to be set aside for worship or if you believe the traditions of the Christian Church through the centuries to be normative, you will choose the first day of the week for that principal time of worship.

What you believe determines not only what you do, but also how you look at a variety of issues, questions, challenges, and problems that are a part of the life and outreach of every congregation.

This book is an examination of twelve of these questions. From this writer's perspective the time has come to challenge the conventional wisdom on each of these questions. This book represents an effort to offer a different perspective on a dozen different questions. It is written from the perspective of a "contrarian." It is based on twenty-eight years of experience in working directly with congregations from four dozen different religious bodies, plus several score independent or nondenominational churches.

The first chapter suggests it is far more difficult than is popularly believed to build and maintain a high degree of diversity within the membership of a worshiping community. The second chapter argues that expectations have a tremendous impact on performance. The third overlaps the second by contending that what you count is what you will reward. The fourth chapter offers an introduction to the widely neglected concept of generational theory as one reason why it is unwise to treat everyone the same.

The fifth chapter proposes that the rate of population growth in a community may rank no higher than eleventh among the factors that determine whether or not a specific congregation will experience numerical growth. The sixth chapter is a plea to update obsolete standards and criteria in deciding how much space is needed. The seventh chapter advises those concerned with limiting tenure to look at the importance of the learning curve. The eighth chapter is an attempt to explain why so many mergers produce disappointments. The ninth chapter suggests that churches are largely exempt from the doctrine of the economy of scale. The tenth chapter describes why it may be difficult to transform a protest movement into a worshiping community. The eleventh chapter suggests the expectations projected on theological seminaries often are excessive. Finally, the last chapter argues that too often evaluation is suggested as an excessively simplistic course of action and that the reasons behind the call for evaluation should determine the procedures to be utilized.

This book represents a challenge to conventional wisdom. If this author is free to issue that challenge, the reader also is free to challenge every sentence in this book. I hope you have as much fun doing that as I did in writing it!

Is There a Price Tag on Diversity?

"Every pastor should long for the day when that congregation represents a microcosm of the nation's population," declared the seminary professor while lecturing to a group of ministers who had come for a three-day event combining Founder's Week, continuing education, inspiration, renewal of old friendships, challenge, hope for grist for the sermon mill, and a chance to get away from that telephone back home.

"The membership of the ideal parish in today's world consists of a cross section of the population," continued the professor. "Whether you look at that congregation in terms of age, the level of educational attainment, race, nationality background, gender, income levels, or social class status, the reconciling parish will be a place where God's children come together across the barriers sinful human beings have erected to separate people into a series of compartments. God calls every parish to be a reconciling community and that means being a completely inclusive parish!"

This challenge was greeted by a mixture of affirmation, envy, questions, longing, approval, awe, doubts, regrets, indifference, and skepticism from among the pastors who attended that lecture.

"Do you mean every parish also should include a broad range of diversity in terms of theology and biblical interpretation?" questioned one minister.

"Yes, within limits, of course," replied the speaker. "We already have seen it is possible for Catholics, Presbyterians, Episcopalians, Baptists, Methodists, Lutherans, and people from dozens of other denominations to come together to worship the same God in an ecumenical service and to pray together in the name of the same Christ. That's happened on thousands of occasions all across the country during the past quarter century. Why can't that happen every Sunday morning in every church?"

Three answers can be offered to that question. The most highly visible answer is that something resembling this scenario does happen every Sunday morning in scores of Protestant churches in both the United States and Canada. A Sunday morning survey of the people present in these congregations would reveal the worshipers include: (1) individuals who were reared in Roman Catholic, Unitarian, Congregational, Methodist, Presbyterian, Episcopalian, Lutheran, Baptist, Christian, Reformed, Churches of Christ, and other religious bodies; (2) substantial numbers of Anglos, Blacks, Hispanics, Asians, and other nationality groups; (3) people from a broad range of educational, economic, and social class backgrounds; (4) all ages; and (5) both males and females.

The vast majority of these congregations that meet all these qualifications are filled with "new Christians" who can identify the time and place when they first truly accepted Jesus Christ as Lord and Savior. Typically the leaders identify this as a "spirit-filled church" that is open to all and does draw from all denominational, nationality, ethnic, racial, social class backgrounds, and age cohorts.

Whether these churches can and do attract a broad range of Christians in terms of belief systems is open to question, depending on the criteria used to define who is a Christian. If the definition is "only someone who believes as we believe," it is self-evident these congregations can and do reach all Christians. (See the fifteenth chapter of the Acts of the Apostles for an earlier debate on this subject.)

The second answer to this lecturer's question has been widely and hotly debated by members of the church-growth movement and their adversaries. It is called the homogeneous unit principle and suggests that numerically growing churches are most likely to be reaching, attracting, serving, and assimilating new members who bear a remarkable resemblance to the people who already are members. Sometimes this is simply referred to as the confirmation of the old adage that birds of a feather flock together. People do tend to socialize with those who share common life experiences and other common characteristics. The big exception, of course, is those congregations that are built largely or entirely around shared religious experiences and a shared belief system, and where interpersonal relationships play only a minor role as organizing principles. In some of these churches, for example, the need for a common language is of minor importance as an interpreter translates the words of the preacher to the congregation. It may be more difficult, however, to make a meaningful hospital visit or to conduct a pastoral call across a language barrier.

Despite the dismay and the objections of those who attack the use of the homogeneous unit principle as a foundation for any church-growth strategy, scores, perhaps even hundreds, of carefully designed research projects suggest it ranks behind only kinship ties as a factor in determining who joins which church—and, of course, some will argue that kinship ties represent the number-one expression of the homogeneous unit principle. The application of this principle is most clearly visible in black, Asian, and various immigrant congregations. The closest to an exception are the smaller, largely Anglo, and often upper-class congregations that resemble a social protest movement (see chapter 10) and continue to maintain a high level of agreement on (a) what is the number-one issue and (b) who is the common enemy. Some advocates of this concept would point to those organizing principles as evidence that they also reflect the homogeneous principle.

The third answer to the challenge raised by this lecturer is widely neglected and deserves more attention from those concerned with the parish ministry. What do you believe is fair to expect of the typical pastor?

While this may sound either paradoxical or irrelevant, some theological seminaries are relatively restrictive in their admission requirements in terms of educational background, language skills, dress codes, age, work habits, behavior requirements, psychological characteristics, belief systems, and social skills. Given these restrictions on admissions, is it realistic to expect these theological seminaries to be able to prepare graduates to serve a highly diverse collection of people? (See chapter 11 for other questions about the realism of the expectations placed on the theological seminaries.) Or should seminaries not be perceived as socializing institutions?

Far more serious, however, is the question of what are the expectations that should be placed on pastors. Is it reasonable to expect every pastor to be able to communicate effectively with people who represent a huge range of political, social, economic, religious, and cultural belief systems? Is it realistic to expect a minister to design and lead an experience in the corporate worship of God that will be meaningful to all who are present, regardless of their place on the theological spectrum? Is it reasonable to expect every minister to be able to provide meaningful pastoral care to people who come from a broad range of cultural backgrounds? (Whom does the pastor hug and whom does the pastor never touch, to use one common and highly inflammable example?) Is it realistic to expect every minister to be able to be an effective Bible teacher when the congregation represents a huge spectrum of differences on biblical interpretation, theological perspectives, and doctrinal views? Is it reasonable to expect every pastor to be able to endure the stress that often is a product of diverse expectations?

In a research project oriented heavily toward United Methodism, which seeks to promote diversity within congregations, James F. Hopewell discovered that pastors who shared a world view common to the world view of the central core of the membership "seem frequently to enjoy a more satisfying relationship with their congregation" than the pastors who expressed a world view substantially different from that of most of the members. Hopewell also reported a positive correlation between the frequency of worship attendance and overlap of world view by the members with the overall orientation of the congregation.[1] In other words, Hopewell found that ministers had an easier and happier experience when their world view coincided with the central orientation of the congregation. The homogeneous unit produces happier pastors.

Those who advocate a high degree of diversity among the members of any one congregation also should recognize that that often places the minister in a stress-producing situation.

Another example of this pattern can be found in the stress frequently experienced by the pastor who for a dozen years happily and effectively served a midwestern congregation composed largely of two-generation households that included one or two employed breadwinners in every family. The "itchy feet" syndrome leads this forty-three-year-old minister to accept a call to a congregation located in one of the retirement counties on Florida's west coast.

After a year or two that migrant minister realizes this really is not a 641-member congregation, but actually is a parish consisting of at least a dozen identifiable congregations including: (1) a congregation of 150 young Southerners who do not share the new minister's definition of the purpose of the church, theological stance, or cultural bias; (2) 175 transplanted, middle-aged midwesterners who moved to Florida for better job prospects, who gained a prominent role in the decision-making processes of this congregation by skills, experience, and initiative, and who welcome a fellow midwesterner as the new minister; (3) 100 members who live here seven months a year, but "vacation" in North Carolina from May through September, and who would be willing for the church to close down during the summer to cut expenses; (4) an overlapping group of several dozen retirees who want an attractive weekday (not week night) program; (5) 200 year-around retirees who place a high value on that hour to two-hour weekly visit from their minister; (6) 25 shut-ins who should be visited weekly; (7) 500 to 600 winter visitors who are not members, but expect a carefully honed sermon as part of that vital worship experience every Sunday morning from Advent to Easter; (8) 41 parents of teenagers who demand a stronger youth program, especially during the summer; (9) 50 New Englanders who would like to recreate here in their retirement years in Florida a replica of the small church they left behind in Vermont or

Maine; (10) an overlapping group of a couple of hundred members who resent the way the winter visitors and the tourists clog up the roads, create long waiting lines at the restaurants and drop only a dollar bill in the offering plate on Sunday morning, but their presence requires the year-around maintenance of this huge building; (11) the majority of both members and winter visitors who want the superb ministry of music, a broad range of choices in the classes in the adult Christian education program, a large and attractive youth group, the skills of a large specialized staff, the extensive weekday programming, and the excellent preaching that are expected to be found in the large congregation along with the intimacy, spontaneity, informality, and fellowship that were the valued hallmarks of that small church "back up North"; and (12) 15 or 20 couples with young children who, thanks to the fact that the wife has taken a full-time job, have a combined family income of $28,000 annually with large monthly mortgage payments that restrict them to perhaps a six-to-ten day vacation once a year and who resent the retired couples in their late fifties and early sixties who own two homes and enjoy a retirement income of $30,000 to $60,000 yearly, part of which comes from the rising Social Security taxes paid by these working-class couples.

This can be a congregation that creates a set of incompatible expectations for that recently arrived minister.

The point of this illustration is not to arouse sympathy for ministers who left the Frostbelt for the Sunbelt, but rather to point out the range of expectations that can be generated from within one Anglo congregation that appears on the surface to enjoy a high degree of homogeneity in terms of denominational affiliation, ethnic identification, language, and current place of residence.

Seven generalizations emerge from studies of diversity within congregational life. First, the greater the degree of diversity, the greater the stress on the minister. Second, the greater the emphasis on the religious aspects of life, the easier it is to accommodate diversity while the greater the emphasis on interpersonal relationships, the more difficult it is to retain that high level of diversity. Third, the greater the diversity among the members, the more important the need to enhance the group life of the congregation so everyone who feels that need can find a homogeneous unit group or "home" within that diversity. In other words, diversity usually produces complexity. Those who want life to be simple and easy to understand and who prefer the uncomplicated tend to resist expanding the group life in order to accommodate that diversity.

Fourth, the greater the degree of diversity, the more critical the personality of the pastor as a central cohesive and unifying force. Fifth, the greater the diversity, the more disruptive changes in staff leadership tend to be, so longer pastorates should be part of a strategy for enhancing diversity. Sixth, the greater the degree of diversity, the more essential a consistent "affirm and build" style of leadership by the pastor. Finally, the greater the degree of diversity among the members, the more likely it will be wise to expect that one result will be a broad and highly varied program with an extremely complex schedule and an exceptionally redundant system of internal communication.

A translation of these seven generalizations means it may be difficult to build and maintain a high degree of diversity within congregations that are relatively small in numbers and/or that can offer only a modest program and/or attract new members largely as a result of friendship and kinship ties and/or tend to prefer short pastorates and/or enjoy "choosing up sides" in making decisions and/or prefer simplicity to complexity.

Is it reasonable to expect one minister, or even one ministerial staff with two or three clergy members plus lay specialists, to serve a highly diverse collection of people in terms of cultural background, age, race, nationality, education, income levels, accumulated wealth, social class, and ethnic orientation? Will the resulting stress on the staff enhance or inhibit ministry?

This observer's experience suggests the answer is yes, that is an attainable goal if (a) all of today's members have joined since the arrival of the current pastor or senior minister, (b) at least 95 percent of what causes the people to come together can be described as strictly religious reasons, (c) that congregation offers a varied and excellent ministry of music, (d) new member-orientation classes run for at least thirty-two weeks before prospective new members are invited to join, (e) the group life is large and offers many choices, (f) the pastor is a gregarious and extroverted personality who also is a superb communicator, (g) a high degree of harmonious diversity exists among the staff members, (h) the congregation is growing numerically, (i) the members are asked to rally behind a specific, attainable, measurable, unifying, and highly visible goal, and (j) the overall level of giving is above average.

The answer probably is no, however, if (a) at least one-half of today's members joined before the arrival of the present pastor, and (b) at least 30 percent of the forces that draw these people together week after week can be described as kinship ties, social cohesion, friendships, shared life experiences, mutual support groups, inter-personal relationships, denominational loyalties, a common nationality, racial, or ethnic heritage, generational ties (see chapter 4), or a widely shared sense of "this is my family."

What are the forces that draw the members of your congregation together week after week and year after year? Do you believe these influence the degree of diversity that can be attained in your parish? What do you believe is reasonable to expect of one minister?

As you reflect on these and similar questions, you also may want to look at how the impact of expectations can influence the acceptable degree of diversity within a congregation.

NOTE

1. James F. Hopewell, *Congregation: Stories and Structure* (Philadelphia: Fortress Press, 1987), pp. 95-99.

What Is the Impact of Expectations?

"We have a relatively simple membership system," explained the Lutheran pastor. "We have six ways that a person's name may be removed from the membership roll of our parish. One, of course, is death. A second is by letter of transfer to a sister Lutheran parish. A third is we may release that member to the care of some other Christian church; the initiatory rite for receiving that person into membership, however, is up to that congregation. Fourth, we can excommunicate, but our parish hasn't excommunicated anyone for at least thirty years. Fifth, names may be moved to our list of inactive members if we no longer have the address, if they have moved out of town, or if they simply have been inactive. Finally, our board of elders may recommend to the church council and the voter's assembly the removal of any name that has been on the inactive list for two years. After two years of attempting to reactivate the inactives, if we're not successful, we remove their names."

"Our system is a little simpler than yours,"

observed the minister of membership from a relatively large and rapidly growing trans-denominational church who was attending the same workshop. "Anyone who fails to attend Sunday morning worship for three consecutive Sundays is taken off our list of voting members unless he or she has an acceptable excuse for being absent."

"Wow!" exclaimed a United Methodist pastor. "I could never get away with that. In our church you have to be absent every Sunday for two years before we can take your name off the membership roll."

"What's your membership and what's your attendance at worship?" inquired the minister from the transdenominational church.

"We report 487 members and last year our average attendance at worship was 176," replied the United Methodist minister.

"We have 283 voting members and currently we're averaging a little over 930 at Sunday morning worship, about 680 Sunday evening, and between 600 and 700 on Wednesday evening," retorted the second minister.

"What are your requirements for becoming a member?" asked the Lutheran pastor who was stalled between awe and envy as he heard those numbers.

"We have eight requirements for full voting membership," explained the minister of member-ship. "First, you must attend every Sunday morning for at least six months before you can ask to be considered for membership. Second, when you apply, you will be examined by a committee of elders who will question you about your faith and commitment and about whether you accept Jesus Christ as your personal Lord and Savior. Third, you're expected to be present for worship every Sunday evening and Wednesday evening as well as every Sunday morning. Fourth, you must be an active and regular member of a group engaged in the study of the Scriptures on a weekly basis. Fifth, you must tithe and return that entire tithe to the Lord through this church. If you want to contribute to other charitable causes, that is perfectly acceptable, but that must be above and beyond your tithe. Sixth, you must agree to serve as a volunteer in the ministry of our church. That can be as a teacher or as an usher or as a host on a bus or whatever fits your gifts, but all members must be engaged in doing ministry. Seventh, if you've been divorced, you cannot be remarried if your first spouse is still alive. Finally, you must abstain from the use of tobacco or alcoholic beverages."

"If we adopted and enforced those rules, we would be a four-member church," observed the United Methodist minister, "and that would give us a far more impressive worship attendance-to-membership ratio than you report."

"What are your requirements for those who are asked to be elders?" inquired one of the two Presbyterian ministers in the group.

"We obey Paul's instructions on that as we find them in the letters to Timothy and Titus," explained the minister of membership. "We have, for example, a wonderful Christian man, who is one of our outstanding leaders but is ineligible to be an elder because he has a six-year-old daughter."

"Why would that disqualify him?" demanded the Lutheran minister who saw himself as the pastor of a theologically conservative parish that carefully followed the Holy Scriptures.

"If you read the first chapter of Paul's letter to Titus, the sixth verse requires the children of elders to be believers," came the response. "We are a believers' baptism church and a six-year-old is not yet old enough to be baptized as a believer, so her father does not meet the New Testament requirements to be an elder. We are convinced this man qualifies in every other respect except this one, and when his youngest child is baptized, I expect he'll become an elder."

This discussion not only illustrates the vast differences among Protestant congregations in the definition of membership, but also introduces one of the most useful conceptual frameworks for understanding the differences among expectations.

What Do You Expect?

For this discussion Protestant congregations can be divided in two categories scattered along a spectrum. One end of that spectrum is labeled "high-expectation churches" and the other is identified as "voluntary association churches."

Voluntary	High
Association	Expectation

At the right end is the smaller number of churches. These congregations expect a lot of each member. While the details vary, a common beginning point is that prospective new members are expected to offer oral autobiographical accounts of their personal conversion experiences, or at least of their own spiritual journeys, to the whole congregation, or perhaps to the elders or deacons, before they can be considered for membership. It also may be more difficult for a person to be received by letter of transfer from a church of a different denominational family. In addition, many high-demand churches require the new adult member to be baptized (or rebaptized) by immersion, although that person may have been baptized earlier as an infant or child.

A growing number of high-demand congregations neither accept nor issue letters of transfer for members. They believe it is impossible for another congregation to be able to certify that someone meets their standards for membership, and it would be equally presumptuous for them to certify that one of their departing members automatically will meet the membership standards of another church.

Members of the high-demand churches typically are expected to be present for corporate worship at least twice a week, to be engaged in a disciplined and systematic study of the Scriptures, to tithe and to give that entire tithe to the church, to be obedient and responsive to the elected leadership of that congregation, to refrain from unacceptable behavior (such as the use of tobacco or alcohol or drugs or the wearing of revealing garments), and to display by their actions as well as by their prayers a high level of commitment to that congregation. While there are many exceptions to any of these generalizations, the high-demand churches usually oppose abortion on demand, believe in the inerrancy of the Scriptures, place a high priority on foreign missionary endeavors, and may not display a strong sense of denominational affiliation or loyalty.

By contrast, many more Protestant congregations fit into a second category that can be identified simply as the "voluntary churches."

While this point can be pushed too hard, the churches in the right half of this spectrum tend to be more conservative on many issues while the congregations scattered along the left half of the spectrum often are more liberal and related to a long-established denomination, *but many exceptions exist at both ends of the spectrum.*

These congregations display more of the characteristics of the voluntary association, in which each member retains the right of withdrawal, than of the closely knit and highly disciplined covenant communities that are found among the high-demand churches.

The voluntary churches usually ask prospective new members to respond in public with one- or two- or three-word sentences to questions on commitment when uniting with that congregation, rather than to offer a public testimony of their faith. In most voluntary churches it is relatively easy to be received into membership by a letter of transfer from another congregation, sometimes even without a public reaffirmation of vows. Every member is expected to attend corporate worship every Sunday morning in the voluntary church, but on the typical Sunday between one-third and two-thirds do not live up to that expectation. Rarely are they reprimanded and seldom are these absentees subjected to church discipline as long as they attend at least 10 percent of the time. Tolerance of diversity, rather than an unswerving commitment to a clearly articulated doctrinal statement, is frequently a mark of the voluntary church.

Some of the more articulate members of the voluntary churches declare, "No one can tell me what I must believe, what I must do, or how much money I should contribute to the church. Those are all matters that are between God and me, not between the minister or the elders and me!"

A substantial majority of the members of the typical voluntary church do not tithe in the sense of giving one-tenth of their incomes to the churches of which they are members. Many of those who do tithe give a portion of that tithe to their congregations and contribute a substantial portion of their incomes every year to a variety of religious, educational, charitable, and philanthropic causes. It is not uncommon for the pastor of the voluntary church to allocate a portion of his or her tithe to causes beyond that congregation. An impressive number of the members of voluntary churches regularly contribute to parachurch organizations and to television evangelists as well as to community causes.

One of the distinctive characteristics of the churches close to the voluntary association end of this spectrum concerns the right of withdrawal. Most high-demand churches view membership as a three-way covenant including God, the member, and that congregation. Therefore, it is impossible for a member to withdraw unilaterally. All withdrawals and dismissals must be acted on by the elders and/or the governing board. By contrast, many members of the voluntary association type congregations are insistent they have a full, complete, and unrestricted right to depart whenever they wish and no one has the right to challenge or question their decision to leave. The leaders of the high-demand churches believe they have an obligation to discipline errant members.

Members of the voluntary church, and especially the leaders, are more likely than the members of the typical high-demand church to belong to other voluntary associations (service clubs, lodges, the PTA, garden clubs, professional associations, 4-H clubs, political parties, YMCAs, veterans' organizations, or civic associations). Not uncommonly, an adult male member of a high-demand church might observe, "My life is built around three points: my family, my church, and my job." By contrast, the man who belongs to the voluntary church is more likely to explain, "It seems like I'm never home evenings. My job often keeps me at the office or takes me out-of-town one night a week, Monday night is football, Tuesday I go to my service club (or lodge or civic association), Wednesday night I bowl, Thursdays my wife and I go square dancing, Friday evenings we're usually at the school with the kids for some program or game, and Saturday night we usually go out to eat. It's hard to work in all those meetings at the church that I should attend."

The voluntary church often provides much of the volunteer leadership, both lay and clerical, for denominational activities. Again, while there are many exceptions, the voluntary churches tend to be more involved in denominational programs than are the high-demand churches. The presence of the latter sometimes is most visible in a denominational debate on a controversial social action issue or in the growing number of caucuses that are pressuring for a return to the Bible or in the battles over the control of denominational boards and agencies.

To return briefly to the theme of the previous chapter, the high-expectation churches often can bring together a more diverse collection of people and meld them into a worshiping community more easily than can the voluntary association type of church in which interpersonal relationships and personal preferences are more powerful forces.

While the foregoing does not constitute an exhaustive list of the characteristics of either category of churches, it will introduce the reader to the concept. High-demand churches can be found most frequently in the Wisconsin Evangelical Lutheran Synod, the Seventh-Day Adventists, the Presbyterian Church in America, the Missionary Church, the Churches of Christ, the Christian Reformed Church, the Christian Church, the Conservative Baptist Association, the Church of Jesus Christ of Latter-day Saints

(Mormons), the Assemblies of God, the General Association of Regular Baptist Churches, the Associate Reformed Presbyterian Church, the Evangelical Free Church, or the Baptist General Conference.

One is more likely to encounter voluntary churches wearing denominational labels such as the United Church of Christ, the Presbyterian Church (USA), The United Methodist Church, the Christian Church (Disciples of Christ), the Unitarian Universalist Association, the United Church of Canada, the Episcopal Church, the American Baptist Churches in the U.S.A., and the Evangelical Lutheran Church in America.

Some of the smaller and younger denominations report their churches tend to be located along the right half of that spectrum toward the high-demand end, but many have drifted to the left toward the voluntary association end.

The natural tendency appears to be for completely new denominations to emerge at or near the high-demand end of this spectrum and gradually drift toward the voluntary association end. That pattern also can be seen in scores of independent or nondenominational churches following the replacement of the minister who founded the church.

In recent years literally hundreds of congregations affiliated with one of the old-line Protestant denominations have begun an intentional and systematic effort to move back toward the high-demand end of that spectrum. This migration to the right usually began after the arrival of a new minister and rarely has a serious long-term impact unless that pastorate lasts for more than seven to ten years.

Back in the late 1960s and early 1970s a big debate divided the Lutheran Church–Missouri Synod on whether or not it should continue to move in the direction of becoming a voluntary church or return to its earlier history as a high-demand church. A similar debate is now going on in several other denominations, including the Southern Baptist Convention and the Roman Catholic Church.

Denominational mergers almost invariably tend to move the new merged denomination toward the voluntary association end of that spectrum. This is the least troublesome way of producing the accommodations required when different polities, traditions, belief systems, definitions of the ordained ministry, cultures, and organizational structures are brought together. That movement in the direction of enhancing the voluntary-association nature of the church often results in the creation of a dissident group that wants to move toward the high-demand end of the spectrum. That shift in the orientation of the new merged denomination may also produce some disappointments in terms of money for missions, membership growth, and sense of cohesion.

What Do You Believe?

Before moving on to look at some of the implications and values of this concept, four questions merit consideration.

First, do you believe this is a useful concept for identifying the differences among congregations, and especially among those that carry the same denominational affiliation?

Second, do you agree that the natural tendency of Christian congregations is to drift toward the voluntary-association end of this spectrum? Or are you convinced the passage of time encourages Christian congregations to move toward the high-demand end of that spectrum?

Third, and perhaps most important, do you believe the location of a congregation on this spectrum will influence its priorities, values, goals, and culture as well as the response of the members? Or do you believe the values, actions, attitudes, and goals of the members determine where this congregation will be located on this spectrum? Which has the *greater* influence on the other? Does the congregation influence the member's beliefs and behavior? Or does the member influence the congregation?

Finally, what do you believe is the impact of the pastor on where a congregation is located on this spectrum? Where will the impact of the new pastor be greatest? In the long-established small church? Or in the very large congregation? In a new mission? Or in a long-established congregation regardless of size? In a black congregation? Or in an Anglo church?

Your responses to those questions will influence how you look at the role, life, ministry, and outreach of your congregation. This can be illustrated by a dozen questions that come up repeatedly in congregational policy-making circles.

1. "We're a 500-member congregation and we plan to build a new sanctuary. How large should it be?"

Part of the answer, of course, will depend on whether the Sunday morning schedule will call for one or two services. If one assumes, for purposes of this discussion, the plans call for one worship service on Sunday morning, the church at the high-demand end of the spectrum may need to build to seat 700 to 1,000 worshipers. The congregation at the voluntary association end of that spectrum might be wise to build to seat 250 to 300.

2. "How many sessions should we require for our orientation class for new members?"

The voluntary association type of church may be content with one to three sessions with each group of new members. The high-demand church may require 24 to 45 sessions to be able to indoctrinate new members into the culture, values, traditions, history, expectations, and life of that congregation.

3. "How many program staff members will we need to be adequately staffed for a church of our size?"

For the 500-member congregation averaging 300 at worship the answer may be two, while for the 500-member congregation averaging 800 at worship, the correct answer may be six or seven.

4. "How much of our total member giving should we be expected to allocate to missions and benevolences?"

In the high-demand church that figure often is between 25 and 50 percent while in voluntary association type churches it usually runs between 10 and 16 percent.

5. "Should we offer parents with younger children the chance to be in worship while their children are in Sunday school?"

A frequent answer in the voluntary association type of church is, "If we don't, the church down the street will offer that choice, and they'll go there rather than come here." In the high-demand church the question may not even arise since everyone is expected to attend *both* Sunday school *and* worship *every* Sunday morning.

6. "That church over there had excellent results with a professional fund-raiser. They went way above their goal. Should we hire the same person for our capital funds drive?"

If that was a high-demand church that had such an enviable experience, the voluntary-association congregation may discover that fund-raiser's techniques are incompatible with the culture of the voluntary-association congregation.

7. "Should we develop a zone plan to improve the care of our members and to enhance our internal communication?"

The high-demand congregation may find it easy to organize a zone plan or undershepherd system that creates a close and continuing oversight relationship with 80 to 90 percent of the members. The voluntary church usually will find it requires far greater effort to organize and maintain such a system, and perhaps one-third or more of the members will not be covered by it.

8. "What proportion of our members can we

expect to participate in the group life of our congregation?"

The high-demand church is able to include three-quarters to nine-tenths of its adult members in face-to-face groups, including Sunday school classes and weekday Bible study programs. The voluntary church rarely is able to persuade as many as 40 percent of the adult membership to be part of continuing weekly face-to-face study and/or sharing groups.

It is only a slight exaggeration to suggest that in the high-demand churches the claims of the community have priority over the autonomy of the individual, while members of the voluntary churches believe the autonomy of the individual takes precedence over the claims of that worshiping community.

9. "That new church out on the edge of town has three buses it uses to pick up children for its Sunday school. Shouldn't we do the same?"

Most bus ministries to pick up children from unchurched families for Sunday school are operated by high-demand churches. Some of them enlist a large cadre of dedicated and hard-working volunteers by explaining, "The only thing that stands between these children and hell is our church. Will you help save these children from going to hell?" Most voluntary churches would find it difficult to make that plea as a means of enlisting volunteers.

10. "Why do we have such a difficult time enlisting volunteers when that church down the road that draws its members from this same community finds it so easy to attract volunteers?"

Typically, the high-demand churches challenge the members to respond to specific needs, jobs, or issues, usually in or through that congregation's ministry and outreach.

Frequently the voluntary churches challenge the members to respond through the structures of society on issues or needs such as world peace, racism, nuclear disarmament, world hunger, or the unrest in Central America. The challenges heard in the voluntary churches often are more rhetorical, while those heard in the high-demand ones usually are more personal, specific, direct, and less divisive.

Furthermore, as was pointed out earlier, the people attracted to the voluntary type church usually reserve the right to determine their own degree of involvement rather than to allow the church to set those standards for each member.

11. "My neighbor tells me their congregation's budget averages out to $2,300 per member. Our church is made up of a wealthier group of people; why is ours so low?"

One reason is that high-demand churches may have very high requirements for membership, so the three-hundred member high-demand church may have many more contributors than the four-hundred member voluntary association type of church.

A second reason is that the higher the income level of the person, the more likely that individual will direct a larger proportion of total contributions to other than his or her local church.

The third reason is expectations. The per-member giving in the high-demand church frequently is double or more than it is in the voluntary church of the same size. The high-demand churches emphasize stewardship and often expect that the member's entire tithe will be returned to the Lord via that church. The voluntary churches often find it necessary to engage in fund-raising programs in order to pay all the bills.

12. "My neighbor, who is a member of a high-demand church, is always talking about becoming a better Christian. How come I don't hear our minister encouraging us to become better Christians?"

Typically, the high-demand churches teach a message that encourages people to become better Christians. By contrast, many voluntary churches teach that when one accepts Jesus Christ as Lord and Savior, one is by definition a Christian. Grace, not works, is the central theme. Paul and Martin Luther both identified professing Christians as "saints." Sainthood is a free gift from a loving God.

It is not uncommon for pastors in voluntary association type churches to advise members, "You're either a Christian or you're not. All of your efforts to become a superior Christian will not change your status in the eyes of God. Your call as a Christian is to be faithful and obedient, not to be superior to other Christians."

At this point the reader may interrupt, "All this says is that the spectrum you described earlier represents a self-fulfilling prophecy. The high-demand churches become high-demand churches by projecting high expectations to their people and the people respond to those expectations."

That is true, but that is not a complete picture. Also at work here is a self-selecting process by both the clergy and the laity. People searching for a new church home who want to be in a high-demand church tend to keep looking until they find it. Likewise those who prefer more of a voluntary association type church tend to keep looking until they find that.

Pastors seeking to serve a high-demand church often either find it or attempt to move one somewhere to the left of center on that spectrum toward the high-demand end. Pastors who are more comfortable in voluntary-association type churches tend to end up in those congregations.

The central point that is being emphasized here, however, is that people do tend either to respond to the expectations projected by that congregation or they depart. That is exactly the same lesson taught and followed by hundreds of elementary schools, high schools, colleges, universities, thousands of employers, the Peace Corps, some, but not all, parents, the United States Marine Corps, the California Youth Corps, and scores of other institutions in our society. Those institutions that consistently and clearly project high expectations of people tend to attract those who prefer high expectations. One result is a higher level of performance. A second is those who are not comfortable with the high expectations placed on them soon disappear from that scene. Expectations do make a difference—both in performance and in the kind of person who joins. That is the story of the encounter of the rich young ruler with Jesus.

Questions for Pastors

If you believe expectations influence both performance and the person who is attracted to which church, it may be worth exploring a few more questions directed particularly at pastors.

1. If you have just arrived as the new pastor of a congregation, or if you are considering a call, you may want to raise these specific questions:

a) Where is this congregation located on that spectrum?

b) Where was it several years ago? If it has moved, in which direction is it moving?

c) Where was the previous pastor located on that spectrum? To the left or to the right of the congregation's location?

d) Where do you see yourself on that spectrum in relationship to both your predecessor and to the congregation as a whole? What are the implications of any differences?

2. If you are the pastor of a congregation at or near the end of the voluntary association end of that spectrum, how do you seek to motivate people? By loyalty? By the law? By high expectations? By rewards in heaven? By enabling them to become better Christians? By love? By grace? By guilt or fear? By concern for others? Through a sense of obligation to this church? By thanksgiving?

3. If you are the pastor of a congregation that is on the high-demand side of the center of that spectrum, what do you say to prospective new members about the expectations of them? If many of the older longtime members joined back

when this was much closer to the voluntary association end, does this help explain some of the conflict between newcomers and old-timers?

4. If you do decide to attempt to transform a voluntary church into a high-demand congregation, will you begin by changing the rules, traditions, customs, and expectations? By first helping transform the members? By changing the criteria for membership? By finding new leaders who want the church to become a high-demand one? By seeking a flood of new members who want to become part of a high-demand church?

What if it works? What will happen to those members who chose this congregation on the assumption that it was and would remain a voluntary church? Will they be required to change? Or expected to find another church home? Or is it assumed that they will simply disappear?

5. What do you believe your congregation is called to be and whom is it called to serve? What is your doctrine of the church? Is the church for those who have little to give? For the poor, the maimed, the lame, and the blind (Luke 14:13-14)? Or is the church only for the saved? Only for those who can respond to the requirements of the high-demand church? Would it be best to remain true to what you understand is the distinctive role of this congregation in this community? How widely shared among your leaders is a common response to those questions?

6. Do you feel pressures to move what you perceive to be a voluntary association type of church toward a high-demand style?

Pastors of voluntary churches are subject to a great many pressures to attempt to transform that congregation into a high-demand community of called-out, highly committed, and disciplined members. These pressures come from a few unusually articulate members, from the highly visible models of high-demand churches, in Asia, Africa, and South America, from the pastor's own study and reflection, from much of the contemporary literature that exalts such churches, from seminary training, and from repeated references by members to "that new and rapidly growing high-demand church out on the edge of town."

7. How much overlap exists among (a) the lay leadership definition of the proper place on that spectrum for this congregation, (b) your definition of where it belongs, (c) the impression left by your predecessor, and (d) the denomination's expectations of congregations?

If your denomination projects strong and clearly articulated expectations of congregations, what is the most clearly defined and frequently referred to expectation: (a) financial support of the denominational program, (b) congregational support for the pastor, (c) lay involvement in denominational programming, (d) baptisms, (e) an increase in the number of members, (f) involvement in issue-centered ministries (sheltering the homeless, feeding the hungry, abortion, civil rights, American foreign policy), (g) innovation in ministry, (h) enhancement of the spiritual journey of the members, or (i) interchurch cooperation? Does any conflict exist between these priorities in expectations and the self-imposed expectations of the members?

8. In operational terms what are the expectations projected by your congregation? Can you detect a relationship between expectations and the way the people respond?

This can be illustrated by several specific examples.

a) Does your Sunday morning schedule suggest you expect people to be present for three hours? Two? Only one hour?

b) If you have combined seventh graders into the same group (choir or youth fellowship) with eleventh and twelfth graders, do you believe it is reasonable to expect most of the older youth to participate regularly?

c) If you receive a special offering on Sunday morning, do you expect people to be generous in their response without being told in advance what the purpose is and/or the goal that has been set for this congregation?

d) When you need additional Sunday school teachers, do you expect people to volunteer in response to an announcement from the pulpit or do you approach prospective teachers on a one-to-one basis?

e) Do you expect newcomers to your community to come to your church on their own initiative? Or do you make a point of extending a redundant series of invitations to all newcomers?

f) If you schedule two worship services for Sunday morning, do you expect to reach and serve more people by offering people a choice of two different formats or orders? Or do you believe a choice in time is all people expect? Or should the range of choices be expanded to include two different orders of worship? Or two different sets of hymns? Or two different choirs? Or two different preachers? Or two sharply different types of worship experiences?

9. Most important of all, do you believe Christianity is a high-expectation religion or a low-expectation faith?

What you believe about the power of expectations, and how you act out those beliefs about expectations, may be the most influential single factor affecting the personality, role, place in the general community, style of parish life, and priorities of your congregation.

What Do You Count and Reward?

"We place a great emphasis on reporting the number of baptisms," explained a man who is the director of missions for an association in the Southern Baptist Convention. "Some of us are convinced that is the most important single indicator of what's happening in our churches. For the past several years we've been averaging about a thousand baptisms a day for the entire Convention."

"How old are these people when they're baptized?" inquired another member of the group. On this Thursday morning of a five-day workshop for three dozen denominational executives the topic under discussion was, "What do you reward?" The point of the discussion was that every denomination tends to count what it believes is important in the life of the worshiping community. Unless it is counted, it is difficult to reward it. Every denomination asks certain questions of every congregation. The questions asked define what can be rewarded. The answers that produce commendation, praise, and other rewards communicate to congregational leaders what denominational leaders believe is important. Thus the question that evoked this discussion was, What do you count and what do you reward?

"We baptize at all ages," replied this director of missions as he turned to page 21 of *The Quarterly Review*, "but most of the people we baptize are older children and youth and young adults. In 1987, for example, we reported 338,495 baptisms, down from 363,124 in 1986. More than 37,000 of these were children under age 9, another 63,836 were age 9-11, while the largest single group was composed of the 79,900 youths we baptized. The grand total included 75,282 young adults in 1987 plus nearly 70,000 other adults."

"Those are impressive numbers," observed a United Methodist district superintendent. "After you allow for the differences in how we define who a member is, your denomination is about a fourth larger than ours, but it's been several years since our total baptisms reached even 200,000. If we kept up with you, we would be reporting 275,000 baptisms a year."

"That explains why we're a younger denomination than you are," interrupted the director of missions. "You're more oriented toward mature adults while we Southern Baptists place a great emphasis on reaching younger families."

"I'm not sure that really explains it," replied the Methodist D.S. as she shuffled through some papers on the table in front of her. "To get back to the question, I guess we place a great emphasis on counting and rewarding the churches that pay their apportionments in full. Twice a year I list in my monthly newsletter those churches that are up-to-date on paying apportionments. I know some superintendents who do that quarterly."

"That's why we're growing and why you are shrinking in size," needled the director of missions with a big smile. "Hardly anyone joins a church to help pay apportionments, but a lot of people do come to church to be baptized or to have their children baptized."

"Why do you place such a high priority on counting baptisms?" inquired a Lutheran.

"Matthew 28:19," came the immediate reply.

"We agree baptisms are important, but we also place a high priority on planting new missions," explained a man from the Wisconsin Evangelical Lutheran Synod, "so we also keep a careful record of how many new churches we start every year. During the middle part of the 1980s we averaged about a dozen new missions every year, but in 1987 that figure was down to only eight. In 1984, however, we started nineteen new missions."

"That is an impressive record," reflected a bishop from the Evangelical Lutheran Church in America. "Given the fact we have approximately thirteen times as many confirmed members as you report, we would have to start 160 new missions every year to keep up with you folks. I don't think there is any one fact or statistic we place at the top of the priority list in terms of importance. We're concerned about baptisms, confirmations, new missions, and a lot of other things. I guess we also are like the Methodists in paying a lot of attention to how much money the parishes forward to the synod. Since the merger, we've been hurting a little in terms of finances."

What Do You Count?

A reasonable assumption is that each denomination, either at the level of the regional judicatory or from the national headquarters, asks congregations to count and report those numbers that measure what are perceived to be important aspects of congregational life. Several of these are obvious and almost universal, such as the annual reports on baptisms, confirmations or professions of faith, deaths, and member contributions.

Many of these figures, unless a larger context is available, tend to be evaluated in comparison with the previous year. Is the number of baptisms higher or lower than last year's total? Is the total membership figure up or down?

The value of this reporting system could be improved by a few modest changes.

First, and by far the most important, is the recognition that what is counted *and rewarded* conveys to congregational leaders what denominational leaders believe are the most important aspects of congregational life. That may not be the intended effect of the denominational reporting system, but that is an inevitable result. That which is counted most carefully, reported with the greatest publicity, and rewarded with the most praise and commendation will be perceived as the most important aspect of parish life.

What do you count in your reporting system for congregations?

The congregations that report the most baptisms?

Congregations that pay apportionments in full?

The congregations that report a net gain in membership?

The congregations that allocate the largest proportion of all expenditures to benevolences?

The congregations that pay the highest ministerial salaries?

The congregations with the largest number of confirmations or professions of faith?

The congregations that have experienced the greatest positive changes in their internal life and ministry?

The congregations that are most heavily involved in community service projects and outreach ministries, such as feeding the hungry, sheltering the homeless, clothing the naked, and caring for the poor? Does the reporting system encourage these community programs to be perceived by outsiders as completely outside the ministries of worship and education of that congregation? Or does it encourage them to be perceived as an integral part of the religious life of that worshiping community?

The congregations that week after week attract the largest number of first-time visitors?

The congregations that offer the highest quality preaching?

The congregations that report the largest number of members who communed during the past year?

The congregations with the largest proportion of members who are tithers?

What Is Rewarded?

The second question concerns the distinction between counting and rewarding. For example, if the rewards go to the congregations that report the largest number of baptisms or confirmations or the largest total membership or the largest amounts of money contributed to missions, that means the reward system is biased to reward the largest congregations and/or those composed largely of young parents. The congregations with a strong ministry with younger, never-married adults or with senior citizens may look bad by comparison.

If, however, the system used to report back to congregations the results of those annual reports is adjusted to allow for the differences in size among the churches, that will change the reward system. This can be illustrated by four examples.

1. Does the denominational report lift up (a) the congregations that reported the largest number of baptisms or (b) those that report the most baptisms per 100 baptized members? Is the emphasis on the gross number or the rate?

2. Does the denominational report lift up (a) the congregations that allocated the most money for benevolences or (b) those that contributed the most per member or (c) those that reached or exceeded the apportioned goal or (d) the proportion of total expenditures allocated to benevolences?

3. Does the denominational report lift up the congregations (a) that experienced the greatest increase in the number of members, (b) that

reported the greatest percentage increase in membership, or (c) that reversed the numerical decline of the past several years? Which receives the most commendation? The 2,000-member congregation that increased in size to become a 2,100-member parish or the 200-member church that grew to 225 members or the parish that, over the previous five years had declined from 850 members to 450 members, but last year reversed that decline and grew to 465 members?

4. Do denominational leaders encourage pastors to officiate at weddings where both parties are nonmembers? If it does, the annual report form should ask about the number of weddings involving nonmembers. If that practice is discouraged, it may be best to exclude any question on that subject, despite the evidence that can be a significant factor in a congregation's church-growth strategy.[1]

The wording of the questions and the format for reporting back to the congregations will convey what the people at headquarters believe is important and worthy of commendation.

Changing Behavior

A third aspect of this subject is the well-known fact that questions asked *in advance* can change behavior. Thus the reporting system should be seen as a behavior modification system.

Many readers will object to that concept in preference for a completely neutral and objective reporting system. That system does not exist. The question is not whether a bias should be built into the reporting system. Every reporting system has a built-in bias. The critical question is whether the nature of that bias is consistent with the values and goals of those who operate the system and those who are influenced by those values and goals.

Does your reporting system convey the impression that the number of baptisms is more important than the number of dollars contributed to denominational causes?

Does your reporting system reward or punish churches for numerical growth? In some denominations the system for defining how much money will be asked of each congregation has been developed to reward numerical decline and to punish numerical growth. In other cases it is designed to convey the impression that little is asked of small congregations and far more is expected from big parishes.

If your denominational agencies provide direct financial subsidies to congregations, do you increase or decrease that subsidy if the average attendance at worship goes down? If it increases, is the subsidy increased or reduced? What do you reward?

If the goal is to use the reporting system to change behavior in a manner that is consistent with denominational goals, it can be designed to encourage that. Again a few examples will illustrate that.

1. How many new congregations did your congregation start or help launch last year?

2. How many new missions does your church plan to help organize in this coming year?

3. How many new adult Sunday school classes did you start last year?

4. How many do you plan to start during this coming year?

5. What proportion of your total congregational expenditures were allocated for missions last year?

6. What proportion do you plan to allocate for missions in this coming year?

7. How many new members did you receive by letter of transfer last year?

8. How many do you expect to receive during this next year?

9. How many circles are in your women's organization now?

10. How many new circles do you plan to organize this coming year? What age group of potential new members will you seek to reach through these new circles?

11. How many tithers were in your congregation this past year?

12. How many tithers do you expect to have this coming year?

These questions reflect several built-in biases. First is the obvious assumption that more is better. Second is the assumption that every congregation will agree these are useful and relevant concerns. Third is the assumption that every congregation does have at least some control over what it will do during the coming year. Fourth is the expectation that each congregation will use last year's performance as a base for projecting goals for the coming year. Finally, this series of questions assumes that questions asked about last year's performance are being asked too late to affect the previous year's performance, but questions asked in advance can influence behavior.

Who Goes to Denominational Conventions?

One of the most sensitive and politically significant questions to be raised about who or what is counted and rewarded concerns the system for determining who will be delegates to the policy-making gatherings of that regional judicatory and of the national convention or conference or general assembly.

Three overlapping systems can be identified, but several variations exist for each of the three. Historically, the most common one has been based on the assumption that the clergy should be represented far in excess of their proportion of the membership of the denomination. This means all or most or at least one-half of the voting delegates will be drawn from the ranks of the clergy.

A second system is based on the more recent goal of granting a voice to the laity. Typically this calls for approximately one-half of the delegates to be drawn from among the laity and one-half from the clergy.

The third system is based on the assumption that the primary basis for selecting delegates to the annual convention of the regional judicatory should be congregations. This means the regional judicatory is perceived as a federation of congregations, not a collection of people. Thus the purpose is to represent congregations (institutions), not people. A common practice is to have each congregation send one lay delegate and one ministerial delegate. Sometimes an adjustment is made to provide for a few extra lay delegates from the very large congregations and/or to allow the larger parishes to send both more ministerial delegates and an equal number of lay delegates. In some cases all the clergy holding ministerial standing in that regional judicatory also may attend with full voting privileges even if many of them are not serving as parish pastors.

All three systems tend to reinforce overrepresentation of (a) the clergy in relationship to the number of lay members of the churches and (b) small congregations. This means the decision-making processes are biased toward being especially responsive to the concerns of (a) the clergy and (b) the smaller congregations. One price tag on this is the challenge by a growing number of the members from the large congregations who recognize the built-in bias in the system and who conclude that other more interesting and rewarding crusades merit their attention. In other words, it is not surprising, if the system is biased toward granting more delegates per one hundred members to the smaller churches, the leaders in the very large congregations will feel alienated from that denomination. This alienation of the leadership of the very large churches from the denomination is an issue that appears to be both more widespread and more visible than it was in the 1950s. In part, of course, it also can be explained by generational theory. (See chapter 4.)

What's the Alternative?

While this may appear to be a radical proposal, a fourth system is possible. This is based on the concept of representing people. Back in the 1960s this received considerable attention as scores of religious leaders eagerly embraced the decisions of the United States Supreme Court in *Baker v. Carr* (1962), *Wesberry v. Sanders* (1964), and *Reynolds v. Sims* (1964) that required both houses of a state legislature to be apportioned on the basis of population.[2] These three decisions turned into the law of the land the rule of "one person one vote." Most denominations, of course, act on the valid assumption they are not bound by those decisions, but some lay leaders are beginning to question the discrepancy.

This possibility of counting people, rather than clergy or institutions, as the primary basis for selecting delegates raises three questions.

The first, which will be evaded here, is a doctrinal debate over the nature of the Christian Church and the role of clergy in the definition of the church. Is the visible manifestation of the church in the clergy? In the people? In institutions called congregations? In some combination of these? In the regional judicatory? In the national assemblies?

The second is what will be the definition of "member," if membership is used as the basis for apportioning delegates? Will it be baptized membership? Active membership? Will the definitions be uniform from congregation to congregation? Or will some congregations be over-represented by the use of lax definitions of membership?

A third question concerns a better way. Would it be fairer and better to use average attendance, rather than membership, as the basis for determining the number of delegates?

While many exceptions do exist, as a general rule the ratio of worship attendance goes down as membership goes up. Thus the one-hundred-member congregation may average sixty-five at worship while the thousand-member congregation may average four hundred and fifty, not six hundred and fifty. Using membership as the base would tend to overrepresent the large congregations.

One indication of how this system would affect representation can be seen by looking at where people went to church in 1986. (See page 60.)

In the Lutheran Church–Missouri Synod, for example, only 5 percent of all parishes average more than 500 at worship, but that 5 percent account for 19 percent of all attenders. Should those parishes be represented by 5 percent of the delegates to the district convention or by 19 percent?

Approximately 70 percent of all United Methodist congregations average fewer than 100 at worship. They account for 34 percent of all worshipers in that denomination on the average Sunday morning. Should those congregations be represented by one-third or by two-thirds of all the voting members at the yearly gathering of the annual conference?

As the table on page 61 indicates, only 20 percent of all congregations in the Baptist

WHERE DO PEOPLE GO TO CHURCH?
AVERAGE ATTENDANCE

Denomination	Under 100 A.A.	100 to 199 A.A.	200 to 499 A.A.	500+
Evangelical Free Church	15%	27%	30%	28%
Wisconsin Evangelical Lutheran Synod	18%	23%	34%	25%
Lutheran Church– Missouri Synod	13%	28%	40%	19%
American Lutheran Church	15%	26%	42%	17%
Baptist General Conference	19%	28%	40%	12%
North American Baptist Convention	20%	28%	40%	12%
Lutheran Church in America	18%	35%	35%	12%
American Baptist Churches	26%	29%	29%	15%
United Methodist Church	34%	28%	29%	9%
United Church of Christ	28%	37%	31%	5%
Church of the Nazarene	37%	30%	25%	8%
Christian Church (Disciples of Christ)	30%	36%	29%	5%

LARGE CHURCHES AND WORSHIPERS

(Large = 200 or more average attendance)

Denomination	A Churches	B Worshipers
Church of the Nazarene	9%	33%
United Methodist Church	11%	38%
Christian Church (Disciples of Christ)	12%	34%
American Baptist Church	14%	44%
Baptist General Conference	20%	52%
United Church of Christ	22%	36%
Lutheran Church in America	22%	47%
North American Baptist Convention	22%	52%
Evangelical Free Church	23%	58%
Wisconsin Evangelical Lutheran Church	26%	59%
American Lutheran Church	38%	59%
Lutheran Church–Missouri Synod	29%	59%

General Conference average more than 200 at worship, but those churches account for 52 percent of the worshipers on the typical Sunday. In the Church of the Nazarene only 9 percent of all congregations account for one-third of the worshipers.

In the new Evangelical Lutheran Church in America approximately 20 percent of all congregations average more than two hundred at worship, but these parishes account for well over one-half of all worshipers on the average Sunday morning. Should they be represented by 20 percent or by 55 percent of the delegates at the annual meetings of the synods?

In choosing delegates do you count the clergy, the people, or the number of congregations?

Which Generation?

Finally, as you look ahead to the future of your congregation and your denomination, which generation do you believe should receive preferences in program planning, in selecting leadership, and in granting authority to policy makers? Do you want to count and reward with authority all the faithful longtime members? Or do you want to give a disproportionately large amount of control to the people who represent tomorrow's members? Which generations will control policy formulation?

In several denominations the decision has been made to give a disproportionately large degree of control to people born before 1940 in the expectation they can and will make the decision that will enable those churches and congregations to reach, attract, serve, and assimilate new generations of members born after 1945. This can be seen in the selection of bishops, executive presbyters, and conference ministers. It is reflected in the process for ministerial placement as well as in the selection of members for important committees.

How well has it worked? One glimpse into the results can be found in some comparative percentages. When asked their religious affiliation, approximately 16 percent of all Americans born before 1924 call themselves "Methodists" as do slightly less than 8 percent of all Americans born in the 1958–65 years. For Presbyterians the parallel figures are 6 percent and 3 percent. For Southern Baptists the picture is more encouraging as 13 percent of all Americans born before 1924 identify themselves as Southern Baptists as do 14.4 percent of those born in the 1958–65 era. For Lutherans the numbers are 9.5 percent and 5.7 percent and for Episcopalians 3.1 percent and 1.8 percent.[3]

Perhaps the basis for selecting leadership has nothing to do with those trends. Perhaps the primary factor among many is the differences among those religious bodies in starting new missions to reach younger generations. But that leads back to the question of who set the policies that determined how many new churches would be organized each year.

As you examine the reporting systems and the assumptions behind the process for selecting policy makers in your churches, what do you count? What do you reward? What do you see as the probable results of the biases built into existing systems? Or are you convinced it is possible to build a bias-free system? Or would you rather look into a more interesting topic that discusses the implications of when you were born?

NOTES

1. Lyle E. Schaller and Edward L. Tucker, *44 Ways to Increase Your Church Attendance* (Nashville: Abingdon Press, 1988), pp. 64-67.
2. For a discussion of the impact of these decisions in the churches, see Lyle E. Schaller, *The Tensions of Reapportionment* (New York: National Council of Churches, 1965).
3. Tom W. Smith, "America's Religious Mosaic," *American Demographics*, June 1984, p. 22.

Is the Generation Gap Real?

"It's always easier to follow a good pastor who had an effective ministry than to follow someone who has forced out by a bunch of unhappy parishioners," declared one minister. "I've followed two ministers who were forced to leave before they were ready to move, and now the same cliques that attacked them are after me. Once a group of members develops a high level of competence in firing the minister, they enjoy putting that skill to use! This congregation has earned its reputation as a killer church."

"That's not been my experience at all," commented another minister during this early arrival period at the monthly meeting of the local ministerial association. "Maybe your church is experiencing three consecutive mismatches between the parish and the pastor."

"How could there be mismatches when each one of us was called by God as well as by the congregation to go there?" challenged this harrassed pastor.

"Let me offer another perspective," urged a

third minister. "I'm enjoying a wonderful time in my church, and I followed an unhappy pastorate, but that really was not the fault of either the members or of that minister. My predecessor's predecessor retired after a great pastorate of thirty-seven years. He was sixty-eight when he retired in 1980. When he left, most of the really active members, and nearly all of the active leaders were past fifty. In other words, this was a congregation in which most of the members were born before 1930, and it was served by a pastor born in 1912. They had grown old together.

"He was followed by a very liberal thirty-two-year-old minister born in 1948 who introduced a lot of what were seen as radical ideas. He also attracted a substantial number of new members from his own generation. Less than three years after he arrived, however, he was forced to leave. The congregation was so badly polarized he could not survive," continued this minister who had been born in 1937. "Fortunately for me, our denominational leadership insisted on an eighteen-month intentional interim pastorate with a mature and wise father figure type of minister who helped resolve the conflict. I also come from that generation of ministers who learned back in the 1960s how to serve as a bridge between the traditionalists born in the first three decades of this century and that liberated generation that came along after the end of World War II."

"I don't know what you're talking about," replied the first minister. "What does your year of birth have to do with enjoying a happy pastorate?"

"That's the issue, all right," came the reply. "Do you believe generational theory speaks to the parish ministry? I do. Back in the 1960s I was a campus minister and that is when I first became aware of generational theory. This has helped me more than any other single concept to understand my new role each time I move. Generational theory has helped me understand why I cannot treat everyone the same."

"That's a terrible approach to ministry if you ask me," argued this first pastor. "I've been taught a good pastor treats everyone the same and doesn't play favorites."

"Playing favorites is another subject," retorted this advocate of generational theory. "All I'm suggesting is it helps to understand that the differences among generations are real and it is somewhere between dumb and counterproductive to ignore what we know to be significant differences."

What Are Those Differences?

Five different generations of adults can be found in the churches today. The first of these five is composed of the people born in the 1910–27 era. During those eighteen years a total of 52 million babies were born in America in that era—and in a remarkable display of stability in fifteen of those eighteen years the total was between 2.8 and 3.0 million. This generation of 52 million native-born Americans had their ranks swelled substantially by immigration through the years, so by the end of 1988 approximately 37 million Americans in the 61-78 age cohort were still alive. (Because of their rapidly shrinking numbers this discussion will not include the 7 million survivors of the generations born before 1910.)

The second oldest generation represents the people born in the 1928–42 era. Only 38 million babies were born in the United States during these fifteen years and, while some immigrants from this age group joined them, this remains the smallest of these four generations. At the end of 1988 a total of 34 million Americans in this 46-60 age group were still alive. In a few more years, however, the inevitability of death will cause their numbers to exceed the survivors of that 1910–27 generation.

A third generation consists of the people born in the 1943–55 era—a relatively short time span. On a year-to-year basis this generation experienced huge fluctuations in the number of births—from a low of fewer than 2.9 million in 1945 to a high of over 4.1 million in 1956. A total of 47 million babies were born in the United States during that thirteen-year period. Again, they were joined by immigrants born elsewhere, and at the end of 1988 nearly 42 million from this generation were still alive. It is the largest of these older generations and it also is an extremely influential generation in many churches.

The next to youngest of these five generations of today's adults consists of the 57.5 million babies born in the fifteen years from 1956 through 1970 plus those who immigrated to the United States. Approximately 62 million members of this generation, sometimes labeled the baby boomers, are still alive. In other words, the members of the generation covering a fifteen-year period are nearly twice as numerous as the generation born in the fifteen years of 1928–42 inclusive.

This generation includes the people born at the peak of the baby boom back in 1956–62. The future of several of the old-line Protestant denominations will be heavily influenced by their success, or by their inability to reach, attract, serve, and assimilate members of this particular generation.

The youngest of these five generations is only now moving into adulthood. The only three statements we can offer about this newest generation with a high degree of confidence reflect what we do not know.

First, no one is yet sure whether the beginning date for the emergence of a new generation is 1968 or 1972 or some other year in that period. Conversations with military chaplains, youth counselors, college professors, high school teachers, and campus ministers, plus the results of social surveys do indicate that a new generation is coming on the adult scene.

Second, it still is too early to be able to describe the distinctive characteristics of this generation with any degree of certainty.

Third, it is far too early to even attempt to describe whether this new generation will span ten or twelve or fifteen or twenty years.

So, what do we know?

Clearly the answer is we know the most about the generations that have been around the longest and least about the youngest.

That Patriotic Generation

The generation of Americans who passed through their formative years between 1917 and 1945 grew up in a highly patriotic era. The regional factionalism of the eighteenth and nineteenth centuries had given way to a sense of national pride that flourished during the presidency of Theodore Roosevelt. The sense of national patriotism that was evoked by this nation's entrance into the First World War was reinforced by the adoption of "The Star-Spangled Banner" as the national anthem in 1931, the Memorial Day orations, the parades, the Fourth of July festivities, and other celebrations for the next quarter century. While the nation became seriously divided on American foreign policy in the late 1930s, that division came to an end on December 7, 1941.

To be more precise, that generation of Americans born between 1910 and 1927 experienced a series of unifying experiences that left their mark. The most obvious were an era of national patriotism, the Great Depression, that remarkable expansion of the public school system that produced the expectation that every youngster would at least attend high school for a couple of years, that national emphasis on institutional loyalties that was reinforced during the 1940s and 1950s, and the most popular war in American history, which lasted into the summer of 1945.

This generation also was taught the values of deferred gratification, the dream of home ownership, oral communication skills through the almost universal ownership of radios and telephones, and the sense of independence that is a product of owning your own automobile. That generation, of which this writer is a part, also benefited from the greatest expansion of the American economy in our nation's history. Most were able to retire before the job crunch of the 1980s hit. This generation discovered the American dream was available to everyone as long as they were covered by a white skin, were male, and did not possess any physical or psychological handicaps.

As of today this generation has produced a larger proportion of adult churchgoers than any other generation in American history. This may cause some to ask whether church attendance and patriotism tend to go together. More significantly, this generation grew into adulthood as the largest age cohort in the American population. They enjoyed the impact of being a majority on the political scene as well as in the labor force. This combination of being a big age cohort plus also being the most churchgoing generation in American history meant they had a tremendous impact on the churches during that church boom of the 1950s. They were especially visible and influential in those churches affiliated with the old-line Protestant denominations—and most are still displaying a strong loyalty to the religious body in which they were reared. The aging of this generation of loyal churchgoers explains why death is such a huge factor in the numerical decline of The United Methodist Church, the Christian Church (Disciples of Christ), and the

Presbyterian Church in the U.S.A., but is of lesser significance in the Southern Baptist Convention or the Seventh-Day Adventists or the Mormons.

Today many are feeling the pain that often accompanies the transition from being an influential majority to the role of a largely ignored minority. This can be seen in some congregations founded before 1960 that peaked in size during the 1960s or early 1970s and subsequently began to shrink in numbers. For many of these churches that downward decline has continued, few newcomers born after 1930 have joined, the old-timers continue to dominate the decision-making processes, and life is relatively placid.

In other congregations, however, that long-term decline was reversed a few years ago, usually following the arrival of a new and younger pastor.

All of a sudden, it seems, a flood of new members have come in, most of them born after 1942. They bring a new set of values, expectations, priorities, and demands. This often includes the demand for a voice in policy formulation. All too often that new minister appears to be giving in too easily to the whims of this new generation. A common response by the old-timers is, "It's great to see so many young people in church, but it sure isn't like it used to be around here." A second comment is, "That's great if we can afford it, but who's going to pay the bills?"

The thrifty majority has become a neglected minority. Why must success breed neglect?

Many of those who pay attention to the pronouncements and policies coming out of the national offices of their denomination also feel offended. As the most loyal, patriotic, and churchgoing generation in their denomination's history, they feel neglected by forces they cannot control. This sense of alienation from the religious body of their childhood is especially obvious among mature Roman Catholics, Presbyterians, and United Methodists.

Most of the members of this patriotic generation have retired from the labor force.

This group can be divided into three groups. The majority have decided to retire in the same county in which they were living before retirement or in an adjacent county. A smaller group have left that friendly home environment in retirement, some to be near their children, others leaving their children behind.

A much smaller, but highly visible group, have decided to spend part or all of the year in one of two dozen counties in the Sunbelt. One of the most interesting slices of this retired generation consists of those who have moved into one of the retirement communities in the Sunbelt developed after 1960. As a group they reflect a dozen distinctive characteristics. These mature adults, when they reach retirement, tend to (1) enjoy unusually happy marriages; (2) be persons who looked forward eagerly to retirement; (3) not feel dependent on their children socially, financially, or psychologically; (4) be comfortable making quick decisions—many purchased their home a day or two after coming south to visit a friend, but they had arrived without any intention of buying a home in that community; (5) love the outdoors;

(6) enjoy an above-average, for their age, state of health; (7) display a strong orientation to their own age cohort and do not miss intergenerational friendships; (8) prefer activities that combine competition, sociability, rules, and boundaries (such as golf or bridge) over solitary endeavors or reflection or hobbies that do not encourage or require a heavy emphasis on interpersonal relationships; (9) enjoy an above-average level of personal income and prefer to live in a one-generation household (60 percent of all Americans born before 1835 who survived to their sixty-fifth birthday were living in the same household with one or more of their children); (10) display little interest in the world of work and responsibilities, such as a leadership role in a local church (typically they do not express the same kind of need to be needed that other retirees often display); (11) find it easy to switch denominational affiliations in search for a new church home; and (12) accept and affirm the benefits of cremation far more readily than people from this same generation who continue to live in the community where they worked before their retirement.[1]

From a congregational perspective this generation born between 1910 and 1927 is the first to challenge the churches to develop a systematic and effective effort in new-member recruitment directed toward mature adults.

It also is significant that the Republican members of this generation, when given a choice in the 1988 campaigns for the Republican nomination for the presidency, chose Senator

Robert Dole over the former television evangelist Pat Robertson by a 2 to 1 margin. Mr. Robertson was more successful, however, than Senator Dole in winning the support of the generation born after 1955.

That Unique Generation of the 1930s

A new and radically different generation was born during the 1930s. This generation differed more than any previous or subsequent generation in several respects. (For those who are so inclined, this age cohort can be expanded to include those born in the 1928–42 period. This generation covering fifteen years shares most of these characteristics. It also should be noted that many individuals do not reflect the characteristics of their age cohort. All generalizations about generational theory recognize the existence of individual exceptions.)

This generation married at a younger age than any other age group in American history, and a larger proportion will marry at least once. Demographers expect that 96 percent of the women born in the 1930s will marry compared to the 86 percent of those born in the 1950s.

This generation of women gave birth to their first child at a comparatively young age and had relatively few children after the mother's thirtieth birthday. This was the last generation of parents who did not postpone the birth of the first child by many years. Thirty percent of the women born in the 1930s had at least two children by their third wedding anniversary compared to only 17 percent of the wives born in the mid and late 1940s. The women born in the 1930s also displayed a remarkably high probability of becoming mothers. Twenty percent of the women born in the United States in the 1900–15 era never bore a child, and 18 percent of the women born in the early 1950s will be childless. Only 7 percent of the women born in the 1930s are childless, the lowest proportion of childless women of any generation in American history. This was the last generation of mothers to have a relatively small number of cesarean births (5 percent compared to 24 percent for today's mothers). This was the first generation to have more than a fourth of the marriages terminated by divorce. This was the first generation in which divorce was more likely than death to terminate the first marriage. This was the first generation of women to be employed in large numbers outside the home.

This was the last generation not to be reared before a television set. This was the last generation to complete high school before the pressures for consolidation eliminated most of the small high schools. This was an important socializing influence that improved their skills in coping with huge institutions such as a state university or the United States Navy or a shopping mall, but did not provide as many leadership opportunities per 100 students as were offered in the smaller high schools.

This was the first generation to reach adulthood in a society in which women constituted a majority of the American population. This was the first generation from which a large number of women were elected to public office. This was the first generation to provide a large number of women for military service. This was the first generation to provide a large number of women who responded to the call to the pastoral ministry. This was the generation from which many of the first feminists were drawn. This was also the generation that provided many of the leaders for the early days of the Civil Rights Movement.

This was the only generation of Americans to enter the labor force when the economy was expanding at an unprecedented rate and when life resembled a pyramid rather than a plateau. This was also the last generation in which a substantial number of parents did not enroll their children in weekday pre-kindergarten classes.

This also was the generation that entered adulthood during the last era of growth of several "old-line" Protestant denominations. This was a generation that became parents during the same years as an unprecedented large number of parachurch organizations and nondenominational or independent congregations gained a high degree of visibility. (The 1956–62 era brought (a) the peak years of the largest baby boom in history, (b) the organization of a huge number of parachurch organizations outside the old-line Protestant denominations, (c) the election of Pope John XXIII, (d) the birth of the Civil Rights Movement, and (e) the election of the first Catholic to the presidency of the United States.) This generation was also the first in American history to include a large proportion of interfaith marriages. This generation of parents, like the previous generation, also has watched a large proportion of their children choose a theologically more conservative path in their religious pilgrimage than the road followed by the parents.

Finally, the older members of this generation include the last group of women, except for those born in the 1963–68 and the 1972–74 periods, to enter adulthood concurrently with a large number of men who are two to five years older. Since women usually marry a man who is two to five years older, it is advantageous for a woman who expects to marry to be born during an era when the total number of births has been dropping for several years.

This generation born during the 1928–42 era also was a comparatively small generation. Fewer than 38 million live births were reported in the United States during those fifteen years compared to 43 million in the previous fifteen years and 51 million in the next fifteen years. At least a few specialists in military affairs agree this birth dearth was one reason the Korean conflict did not escalate into a world war. The personnel needed to fight a full scale war had not been born in the 1930s.

Before leaving this question, a word of caution must be offered. This generation has produced many very influential and highly persuasive leaders. Like all of us, they tend to assume their values, goals, struggles, hopes, dreams, and ethical standards are representative of all people. In fact, this was a relatively small generation that was not and is not representative of the general population.

A simple illustration of this is the fact that the people born in the 1930s grew up in a society that taught us it is acceptable to classify people by marital status. One result was a great emphasis on couples classes in Sunday school. Another was the creation of countless groups for single adults. Many of today's never-married adults who were born in the late 1950s perceive the classification of people by marital status as a rude, discourteous, and offensive system.

During the late 1950s, the 1960s, and the early 1970s it was reasonably easy for an urban or suburban congregation to build a large ministry with single adults, most of whom were never-married persons born in the 1928–42 period. One of the attractions of the big singles programs was the possibility of meeting that future spouse.

By the late 1970s the leaders of the ministries with unmarried adults saw the need for a broad umbrella that could cover never-married adults born in the late 1940s and early 1950s, the widowed of all ages, the divorced men who were seeking a new mate, the divorced women who were still recovering from a traumatic divorce, the older, never-married adults born before 1940, the exploited and hurting women who displayed little or no interest in marriage, old men, people with serious personality problems, adults who happened to be between marriages, and a growing number of younger women who held and openly expressed deep hostilities toward any system that classified people by marital status.

Few churches were able to find an umbrella that broad in its coverage. One result was an erosion of the popularity of singles ministries. Another was the emergency of a new wave of young adult groups that included both never-married adults, childless couples, and a few who were currently divorced. A third was the decision to encourage many single adults to join groups composed largely of couples (the most offensively named of these were the "Pairs and Spares"). A fourth result was growing frustration among the veteran leaders of some churches as the size of the singles group dropped from several hundred to a couple of dozen regular participants.

In programmatic terms it also should be noted that back when many teenagers attended small high schools, back before popular music could be *seen* on television, back when very few teenagers had part-time jobs during the school year, and back before the emergence of the shopping mall, it was relatively easy to organize a large, cohesive, and attractive high school group around study, fellowship, and an attractive leader. What were useful central organizing principles for building a youth group in the 1950s rarely are that effective in today's world.

Likewise the young couples class was a re-markably effective entrance into the church for people in the 18-25 age bracket in 1960 when only 28 percent of the women aged 20-24 had never married. Today, when three out of five of those aged 20-24 have never married, the young couples class provides a far narrower entry point.

What had worked so well with one generation created problems when the same organizational principles were applied to three different generations. Perhaps the central point to remember is that the generation born in the 1928–42 period represents considerable discontinuity with *both* earlier and later generations.

The Liberated Generation

The largest age cohort in a population often dominates the larger group. The older members of that generation born during the years 1943–55 dominated the college and university campuses during the 1960s. Many were active in the Civil Rights Movement, led the opposition to established authority, and were committed to the struggle to reexamine old traditions. This generation also provided most of the enlisted personnel for the American military forces in Vietnam. As a group this generation was seen as somewhere between liberal and radical in matters such as respect for authority, the values of deferred gratification, dress, the usefulness of tradition, drugs, the preservation of established elite groups, sex and marriage, political campaigns, and patriotism.

This was a generation that did not fit comfortably into a military organization, but a large proportion of today's military officers are drawn from this generation. Their civilian peers have changed American society just as those who chose a military career have transformed the culture of the armed forces.

Unlike the generations born in the first three decades of this century who were taught by two wars and the Great Depression to place a high priority on survival goals, this generation placed identity at the top of the priority list. "Who am I?" and the search for meaning in life replaces survival as the most important personal agenda.[2]

The younger women from this generation, as they look for a husband who is a few years older, are finding the supply to be limited. For example, the two million women born in 1954, if they seek a husband who is three years older, find only 1.9 million men were born in 1951. In addition, the death rate among young men is nearly twice that of women of the same age. Add in the fact that 200,000 of the male survivors born in 1951 will never marry, and it is easy to explain why a singles group of people in their thirties today will include many more women than men.

This is the generation that produced the recruits for scores of new experimental communities across the nation. These ranged from the homosexual Castro community in San Francisco to rural "back to nature" communes that flourished in the late 1960s and 1970s to the Rajneeshpuram community in Oregon that attracted worldwide attention in the 1982–83 era to various political groups.

This is the generation that created a radical new value system in both Canada and the United States in regard to homosexuality. This is the generation of people who shocked their parents by an openness toward divorce, and some of them subsequently were shocked when their parents decided to terminate their marriage by divorce.

This was the generation that challenged long-established and widely accepted traditions in the colleges and universities, in the practice of medicine, in the use of forbidden words, in what was acceptable dress in places of public assemblage, in what was off limits to the press, in what could be reserved for males only, in the procedures for nominating presidential candidates, in the relationship between tenants and landlords, and in scores of other customs, habits, and conventional behavior patterns.

This included challenging the customs, traditions, rules, and restrictions of religious bodies. One result was that the decades-old pattern in which more Protestants joined the Roman Catholic Church year after year was reversed. The exodus, thanks largely but not completely to this generation, began to exceed the converts.

From the Protestant side of the ecclesiastical fence, which the previous generation also helped lower, the movement was clearly from the old to the new. Many members of this liberated generation, who were reared in one of the old-line Protestant denominational families, left the church in their teens. When they returned, however, many chose to be part of a new congregation. Hundreds of these congregations are not affiliated with any denomination. Others are related to one of the newer religious bodies such as the Assemblies of God, the Churches of Christ, the Church of God in Christ, the Baptist General Conference, the Evangelical Free Church of America, the Seventh-Day Adventists, the various bodies that call themselves the Church of God, as well as other new denominations. Many of these groups refer to themselves as movements or associations or fellowships and reject being labeled denominations.

A New Conservative Generation

While all the returns are not yet in, the evidence to date suggests the emergence of a new generation with many shared characteristics from among those born during and immediately after the peak of the baby boom of the 1956–62 era. It is too early to identify a closing date for being included in this generation, but a reasonable guess would be 1969 or 1970 or 1971.

A total of nearly 60 million babies were born in the United States in those fifteen years of 1956–70, compared to 51 million in the preceding fifteen years, and 52 million born in the next fifteen-year period of 1971–85 inclusive. This is a very large age cohort! The size of this generation has enabled the armed forces to be highly selective in their standards for enlistment. Among other products of this selectivity is the best educated group of enlisted personnel in American military history.

When compared to the 1943–55 generation, this age cohort appears to be far more conservative by most criteria than its older siblings. This can be seen in voting patterns as well as in social surveys of values, attitudes, behavior patterns, hopes, and ethical standards.

This generation includes a disproportionately large number of members who display a conservative view of the world on social, theological, economics, political, and philosophical issues.

In several respects they resemble the people born in the first quarter of this century with their interest in survival goals. The big exceptions to that generalization are that this generation is (1) more liberal on anything dealing with race, sex, marriage, and divorce; (2) less likely to be motivated by the concept of deferred gratification (saving money for a rainy day, abstinence from premarital intercourse, choosing homework over a part-time job while in high school); (3) less likely to be persuaded of the value of working one's way up the career ladder; (4) more inclined to ignore the institutional loyalties of their parents; and (5) less likely to build their identity around their work or their employer (such as a career with one corporation). Not all of these exceptions, however, apply to everyone from this generation of strivers and survivors.

For the most part this generation also displays a high degree of patriotism somewhat similar to that of the generation born in the 1910–27 era.

Members of this generation often take for granted the reforms and the contemporary egalitarianism that represent the victories won by the crusaders from older generations—and some of the old-timers resent that.

This generation of women was the first to find the doors of the military academies open to them. The conservative attitude of many of the young men from this generation surfaced as women enrolled in the service academies in 1976 for the first time in history.[3]

The younger women from this generation live

in a different world when the subject of marriage comes up than the one inhabited by women born in the 1943–55 era. Slightly more than 1.7 million girls were born in 1967, for example. Well over 2 million boys were born in 1964. Thus the 22-year-old women of 1989 or 1990 have a far larger supply of potential husbands than is available to the women born in the early 1950s. Women benefit from being born on the downside of the birth curve while men benefit from being born on the up side of that curve when the issue is finding a spouse.

The people conducting the social surveys taken in the year 2009 or 2010 probably will report a larger proportion of this generation has turned out to be regular churchgoers than is true of the 1942–55 generation.[4]

This generation clearly is attracted to excellent Bible preaching, to large churches that can and do offer a broad range of high quality ministries, to the opportunity to help pioneer the new, to the churches that place a great emphasis on music in corporate worship, and to high quality visual communication. Scores of pastors have identified this as the "sight, sound, and sensation generation." One illustration of the application of this is in new church development. The mission developer seeking to reach the generations born before 1956 often will choose a public school building as a temporary meeting place for the first couple of years. The minister seeking to create a new congregation drawn from the sight and sound generation is more likely to choose a motion picture theater for that temporary meeting place.

Of the four generations described thus far, thanks to changes in immigration patterns and differences in birth rates, this generation has the smallest proportion of Anglos; approximately 87 percent of all Americans born in the 1910–27 era are Anglos compared to approximately 80 percent for the 1956–70 generation and to slightly under 75 percent of all residents of the United States who had not reached their fifth birthday by December 31, 1988. (It should be noted that varying definitions of "white" and "Anglo" can make slight differences among these percentages.) Future-oriented readers concerned with either the public schools or with Sunday school will need to respond to the fact that by the year 2001 approximately one-third of all schoolchildren in the United States will be members of a minority group.

The translation of that into church-growth terms is those denominations that (a) are organizing many new missions and/or (b) include many very large congregations and/or (c) place a premium on high quality biblical preaching and/or (d) know how to exploit the power of music and/or (e) organize new congregations to reach and serve the ethnic minority components of the population are the denominations most likely to be experiencing numerical growth.

Some will argue that the most important issue affecting this generation is the threat of AIDS. Others contend this is the first generation of Americans to perceive voluntary military service as better preparation than college for entrance into the civilian labor force. This generation was born into a world that has experienced the longest period of peace (a period without a major war involving two or more of the great powers of the day) in the Western world since the days of the Roman Empire. This generation also has been taught that visual communication is more effective than oral communication.

What Next?

A new baby boom began in 1977 when, for the first time in six years, the number of live births exceeded 3.2 million. The 1980s have seen the number of births run between 3.6 and 3.9 million annually. This compares to 1970, the last previous year when that number exceeded 3.7 million, and to the birth dearth of 1973–77 when the annual total never reached 3.2 million live births.

While the signs suggest the emergence of a new generation, it is premature to offer specific characteristics of this new age cohort. We do know that a huge variety of people are commenting, "The old systems don't seem to work with this new generation of young adults." These are the people who have been working for years with a passing parade of seventeen-, eighteen-, and nineteen-year-olds. Their ranks, as was pointed out earlier, include high school teachers, campus ministers, military training officers, employment counselors, college teachers, parents, producers of products for that segment of the retail market, youth counselors, and demographers.

Before moving on to a discussion of a few of the implications of generational theory, it should be noted that this is not a new concept. Classical writers such as Homer and Herodotus referred to generational differences, and the Bible repeatedly identifies generational rifts. Observers from different cultures and different generations do not always agree on the definition of a particular generation or on the distinctive characteristics.[5] What has been offered here is a brief introduction to the concept, and it should be clear that universal agreement does not exist for either the beginning or the terminal year for each generation described here, but broad agreement can be found on the existence of these five generations in the contemporary American culture.

What Does It Mean?

Perhaps the most common example of the relevance of generational theory on the American church scene is its usefulness in explaining some of the conflict that may arise over values, priorities, definition or purpose, and allocation of resources when the pastor born during the first quarter of this century is followed by one born after World War II. When that happens it often becomes easy to persuade both the older longtime members and the new young members that the "generation gap" can be real.

A second example was illustrated by the discussion about ministries with adults who are not married. What appeared to be an effective approach to ministry with one generation may not work with younger generations.

A third example is the pew versus denominational headquarters conflict. Part of that conflict is a result of vast differences in values, in the definition of the purpose of the Christian Church, and in priorities. Part of it, however, clearly is a conflict between the perspective of the generation born before 1928 and younger generations. Part of it is a natural and predictable conflict in perspective between "those back in headquarters" and "those in the frontline trenches." Today considerable disagreement exists over whether the frontline trenches are the pews, the pulpits, the picket lines, or the press conferences.

One of the less widely recognized implications reflects the combination of ministerial placement and "dropouts." A growing body of evidence suggests that the largest single factor in explaining why people drop out of church or leave for another congregation without changing their place of residence is a change in pastors. Generational differences often are one component in the mix of reasons behind those departures. Therefore, regardless of whether the system is based on selecting a committee of lay volunteers who will conduct a search for a new pastor or recommendations from a denominational officer or direct appointment by a bishop, it would be wise for the persons responsible for ministerial placement to look at generational theory in that process.

Another implication surfaces regularly in these situations in which a minister is expected to be engaged in cross generational activities. One example is the minister who carries the youth portfolio in that large congregation and also is expected to make one-half of the hospital calls. Another is the navy chaplain who reports to an older generation of superior officers and is responsible for ministry with large numbers of people in the seventeen- to twenty-four-year age bracket. A third is the seminary professor. A fourth is the campus minister.

That is a radically different context for doing ministry than is encountered by the parish pastor who was born in 1947 and is organizing a new congregation with most of the adults coming from among parents born in the 1942–55 era. Most of us find it easier to relate to people from our own generation than to other age cohorts. A common example is the fifty-seven-year old parish pastor who explains, "I quit trying to do youth ministry fifteen years ago." Another expression of this same behavior pattern is called "early retirement." Others simply refer to the "generation gap."

Another part of this perspective on the world is that most of us have more practice "getting along" with people older than themselves than we have in getting along with younger generations. Our parents were our first teachers in helping us perfect our skills in getting along with older people. A few years later we began to expand our skills in getting along with older people as we encountered relatives, neighbors, teachers, merchants, physicians, employers, dentists, barbers, Scout leaders, ministers, and other adults. By age twenty most of us were convinced we had a high level of competence in getting along with people from our own age cohort, a fair level of competence in getting along with older adults, and very limited ability to relate effectively to immature youth and children—most of whom obviously had migrated here from some other planet and clearly are unlike who we were when we were younger.

One example of this tendency of adults to feel inadequate in relating to younger people is that most adults find the size of their friendship circle shrinking after they pass their sixtieth birthday. Most mature adults experience difficulties building relationships with people who are three or four decades younger. Some invest considerable time and energy in reestablishing their relationships with kinfolk and old friends they have not seen for thirty or forty or fifty years, but who represent their own generation.

A great many senior pastors report they find it easier to relate to staff members from their own generation or who are older, but experience difficulties working with younger members of the staff. It is not uncommon for the fifty-three-year-old senior minister to give himself a grade of A- in his ability to relate to staff members under thirty-five years of age, but those younger staff members suggest a grade of C- would be closer to reality.

By and large, people are most comfortable socializing with people from their own age cohort. A few exceptions stand out. Some are unique personalities. Most are people who are obliged for professional reasons to improve their skills in relating to those younger than themselves. That list includes public school teachers, military chaplains, youth directors, college professors, campus ministers, people engaged in direct sales, and case workers in social welfare. The difficulties that older people encounter in relating to younger generations may explain why many engaged in these vocations often move into administrative positions as the years roll past.

For one group of adults generational theory helps explain their role as a "bridge generation." This was highly visible back in the 1960s when ministers and campus pastors born during the 1930s found themselves acting as a communication link between the parents who represented that older patriotic generation and the members of that liberated generation born during and after World War II. For many pastors this was a role-shaping experience.

Finally, the concept of the deference pyramid or pecking order is useful in explaining generational differences. For generations American society has taught people that (1) younger are expected to defer to older people; (2) newcomers are expected to defer to those with long tenure; (3) women are expected to defer to men; (4) employees are expected to defer to employers; (5) people with less education are expected to defer to those with more formal education; (6) people without titles are expected to defer to those who carry impressive titles; (7) people at the lower end of the salary scale are expected to defer to those at a higher salary level; (8) people from small institutions are expected to defer to people representing big institutions; (9) Blacks, Asians, and Hispanics are expected to defer to Anglos; (10) students are expected to defer to teachers; and (11) the laity are expected to defer to the clergy.

The generations born before 1928 tended to accept and reinforce this deference pyramid. The generation born in the 1928–42 era challenged it. The generation born between 1943 and 1955 fought to level that pyramid, although some simply ignored it. Many members of the generation born after 1955 are persuaded the deference pyramid is largely an obsolete if not demonic heritage from the past, but have to live with these three older generations who view it from three radically different perspectives. The typical parish pastor also has to relate to the older three generations, but most of that congregation's future new members will come largely from the fourth of these four generations. It usually is helpful to be able to use a larger context for one's ministry.

Do you believe that generational theory offers a useful conceptual framework for looking at congregational dynamics? Do you believe generational differences are significant in lay-clergy relationships? In building a staff in a large church? In filling vacant positions?

NOTES

1. For a more detailed statement on the distinctive characteristics of these retirement communities, see Frances Fitzgerald, *Cities on a Hill* (New York: Simon & Schuster, 1986), pp. 203-45, and Lyle E. Schaller, *Expanding Ministries with Retirees, Seasonal Visitors, and Tourists* (New York: The United Church for Homeland Ministries, 1987).

2. William Glasser, *The Identity Society* (New York: Harper & Row, 1972).

3. Judith Hicks Stiehm, *Bring Me Men and Women: Mandated Change at the U. S. Air Force Academy* (Berkeley: University of California Press, 1981).

4. One of the reasons for the strong church-going practices of people born during the 1910–27 era is many parents in the first quarter of this century made "loyalty to the church" the number-one value they sought to instill in their children. See Anne Remley, "From Obedience to Independence," *Psychology Today,* October 1988, pp. 56-59.

5. For an introduction to the concept of generational theory and its historical context, see "Generations," *Daedalus,* fall, 1978, issued as vol. 107, 4 of the Proceedings of the American Academy of Arts and Sciences. See also Daniel Yankelovich, *New Rules* (New York: Random House, 1981); Douglas Alan Walrath, *Frameworks: Patterns for Living and Believing Today* (New York: Pilgrim Press, 1987); Richard A. Easterlin, *Birth and Fortune* (New York: Basic Books, 1980); and Fitzgerald, *Cities on a Hill.* See also the training film or videotape by Morris Massey, *What You Are Is Where You Were When.*

What Is the Influence of Population Growth?

"To what do you attribute the rapid growth of this parish between 1983 and 1988?" asked a visitor of one of the leaders of a Lutheran congregation in southeastern Charlotte. "Your attendance at Sunday morning worship more than doubled in that period. Why?"

"We were in the right place at the right time," came the instant reply. "Charlotte was experiencing a population boom during those years, and we were right in the path of it."

* * *

"I predict that when all of those apartment buildings now under construction are completed, we'll be able to reverse our numerical decline," declared a longtime member of First Church as he and a half dozen members stood on the front steps and looked at the residential construction now underway.

* * *

"As part of our church-growth strategy, we have contracted with a private firm to supply current demographic figures and projections from census tracks or zip code areas to any church in our denomination that asks for them," explained a denominational staff member.

* * *

"We need a subcommittee that will gather the necessary population projections for this end of the county," said the person chairing the recently organized long-range planning committee at the Oak Ridge Church. "Anyone ready to volunteer?"

* * *

These comments represent the widespread assumption that a critical factor in parish planning is knowledge of population trends. This parallels the assumption that congregations are more likely to experience numerical growth if located in a community experiencing population growth and may expect to decline if the population is shrinking. This correlation between population growth and congregational growth appears to be so obvious that it is rarely challenged.

What Does the Record Reveal?

Only two reasons can be offered to challenge that assumption. The first is the historical record. An analysis of the statistical data for those counties in the United States that experienced a population increase of 25 percent or more between 1970 and 1980 reveals (a) in a majority of

97

those counties the reported membership of the congregations affiliated with a half-dozen old-line Protestant denominations (American Baptist Churches in the U.S.A., Christian Church [Disciples of Christ], Presbyterian Church in the United States, United Church of Christ, United Methodist Church, and United Presbyterian Church in the U.S.A.) decreased despite that population growth, and (b) in a majority of these counties a majority of the congregations affiliated with these six denominations reported a net decrease in membership. In other words, that decrease was *not* simply a product of a huge drop in the membership of a few churches. It was the result of the numerical decline in many congregations.

What Are the Variables?

The second reason to challenge that basic assumption is based on more subjective data derived from consultations with several thousand congregations over the past three decades, plus an examination of scores of surveys, studies, and reports.

What are the critical factors that accompany numerical growth in congregations? The first three on this list can be documented by a statistical analysis. The next seven clearly are more subjective and are vulnerable to any efforts to demonstrate a single factor analysis.

The first and most obvious variable is that new congregations are far more likely to report numerical growth than are long-established churches. One reason, of course, is that most new missions are launched in communities experiencing population growth. If, however, the analysis is limited to communities experiencing at least a 2 percent annual increase in population, the record reveals that nearly all the congregations founded during the past five years will be growing while a majority of those congregations founded at least twenty-five years earlier will be reporting little or no increase in size. The age of the institution stands out to this observer as the most influential single variable in church growth.

From a denominational perspective this is an easy-to-measure variable. The denominations most likely to report an increase in membership are those in which at least one-fifth of all congregations have been established during the past fifteen years. (*The U. S. Census of Religious Bodies of 1906* reported that in 1906, 40 percent of all Lutheran parishes had been organized within the past seventeen years as had 30 percent of all Congregational churches, 21 percent of all Methodist Episcopal Church congregations, 27 percent of all Presbyterian Church USA churches, 22 percent of all Methodist Episcopal Church, South, congregations, one-fourth of all Northern Baptist churches, one-third of all Southern Baptist congregations, and one-third of all Protestant Episcopal parishes.) The population increase in the United States between 1890 and 1906 was 22.5 million. Between 1970 and 1986 the population of the United States increased by 39 million.

At the end of 1986 The United Methodist Church reported slightly over 2 percent of all congregations had been founded during the past seventeen years. In most of the other old-line Protestant denominations that proportion was between 1 and 5 percent. In several rapidly growing religious bodies that figure ranged from 20 to 50 percent.

Before leaving this subject it should be added that many congregations trace their "current beginnings" back, not to the date of formal organization, but to the date when they moved to the present site and constructed the new meeting place. Thus the eighty-eight-year-old congregation that relocated nine years ago may today closely resemble a new church. This also helps explain why the relocation to a new meeting place often can be a useful component of a congregational revitalization process.

The second variable is the ethnic mix of the population. Thus the Anglo congregation located in a community experiencing substantial population growth, but most of it due to Asians, Hispanics, or Blacks who are moving into housing previously occupied by Anglos, probably will be reporting a decline in attendance, not an increase.

The third of these three measurable variables is the size of the congregation. The larger the congregation, the more likely it will grow. The smaller the number of members, the less likely that congregation will grow. Small congregations tend to be heavily oriented toward care of the membership while larger churches are more likely to offer a variety of entry points for potential new members. In part, this reflects the availability of discretionary resources, but it also reflects the range and quality of programming.

Those congregations averaging more than three hundred at worship are far more likely to experience numerical growth than those averaging fewer than one hundred in worship. "Them that has gits" is the ancient adage that applies here.

To place this in a denominational perspective, the large church denominations, such as the Lutheran Church–Missouri Synod and the Evangelical Free Church, are more likely to grow in numbers. By contrast, a denomination with a strong orientation toward increasing the number of congregations averaging fewer than thirty-five at worship is less likely to report increases in membership for the entire denomination.

The size of the congregation is a far more influential variable in predicting numerical growth than is an increase in the population of the general community.

Before moving on to an overlapping group of seven subjective considerations, a word of caution must be offered. The central thesis of this chapter is not to ignore population trends—just be careful not to give them excessive weight in looking to the future. For the vast majority of congregations the internal factors discussed here are far more influential in regard to numerical growth than external considerations such as population growth or decline. Obviously there are many exceptions. It is difficult to build a big youth program in a community populated largely by retirees. It also may be more difficult for a congregation to experience rapid numerical growth when many people are moving out of town and few are moving in. As will be pointed out later, a high rate of turnover in the population often is more significant than a modest increase or a modest decrease in the total population.

In other words, please do not ignore population growth trends, but do not identify those numbers as the determinative variable!

A fourth variable that is far, far more influential than the rate of population growth or decline is the quality and quantity of the total program. This includes the preaching, the ministry of music, the Christian education program as well as a variety of specialized ministries.

A strong argument can be made that this is the most influential single factor in determining the numerical growth or decline of a congregation. It is placed fourth here for three reasons. First, it is a more subjective factor and more difficult to measure objectively than the first three variables. Second, it overlaps several other factors on this list. It defies any attempt at single factor analysis. For example, recently organized congregations tend to be more sensitive and responsive to the contemporary needs of people than do long-established parishes. Third, a comprehensive program rarely is found except in large congregations, but other factors also influence the growth of big parishes.

A fifth variable, and many experts in church growth contend this should be placed first, is the competence, vision, and gifts of the pastor. One reason for placing it this low is the highly subjective nature of the discussion. In more precise terms it may be more meaningful to focus on the quality of the match between the pastor and that parish. Scores of exceptionally competent ministers have watched as the congregation they were serving diminished in numbers. The most common explanation was that there was a mismatch between pastor and parishioners. Sometimes it was clearly a product of generational conflict. (See chapter 4.) More often, however, it was a mismatch of gifts and needs.

This variable also clearly overlaps the previous point since the minister usually is the most influential force in determining the quality and nature of the total program and ministry of that congregation.

It also should be noted there often is a correlation between the tenure of the pastor or the senior minister and numerical growth. If the current minister has been in that pastorate for five years or longer, and if that congregation has been on a plateau in size or shrinking in numbers, it probably will not begin to grow, regardless of the changes in the rate of population growth in that community, until after the arrival of the next pastor.

This is *not* an argument for short pastorates! That is not the point. The key variable appears to be those first few years of a new pastorate. If a congregation is going to experience numerical growth with the leadership of that minister, the numbers usually will begin to reflect that within the first few years.

In other words, a disproportionately large number of long-established congregations reporting numerical growth began to experience that growth shortly after the arrival of a new pastor.

This is *not* an argument in support of short pastorates for ineffective ministers! This is simply to note the *immediate* impact of a new minister, many of whom stay for decades and the congregation may continue to grow in numbers throughout that very long pastorate, but those first few years usually set the direction for the future.

The sixth, and perhaps an even more subjective variable in church growth, appears to be the basic orientation of the congregation. Those congregations that allocate all or nearly all the resources to taking care of the members tend not to grow. Those that place a high priority on the allocation of resources to identifying, reaching, attracting, serving, and assimilating new members are far more likely to grow. This may be one of the two or three most important factors in explaining why small congregations, which often display a strong member orientation and are convinced they have limited discretionary resources, tend not to grow in size and why big churches are attracting a disproportionately large number of new members.

A seventh variable is the availability of adequate off-street parking. This is (a) more influential west of the Mississippi River than east of it, (b) more important in congregations seeking to reach people born after 1945 than in those parishes largely oriented toward people born before 1940, and (c) especially important for weekday and evening programming. Those congregations in which the central component of the growth strategy is superb preaching usually report that the availability of convenient parking is not as critical as it is to those congregations that have made Monday-to-Friday programming a central drawing card of their church-growth program. People will walk a greater distance on Sunday morning than on a weekday night.

While some will place it higher and others may place it lower on this list, staffing usually is more significant than population trends in determining church growth. The first issue in staffing, as was pointed out earlier, is a good match between pastor and that parish. The second already has been described, the orientation of the staff toward taking care of the members or toward evangelism. The third is competence. The fourth is productivity. (Should this be ranked higher?) Some people are three-to-six times as productive as others. In the same amount of time they can complete more work. A big variable in staffing is the distinction between staffing for growth (which usually requires either a more productive staff or a larger staff) or staffing to remain on a plateau in size or staffing for numerical decline.

A ninth influential variable in determining whether or not a congregation will grow in numbers is the adequacy of the physical facilities. Many congregations that could and should be reaching more people with the good news that Jesus Christ is Lord and Savior are severely limited by the inadequate and/or obsolete building and/or the size of the site and/or the location.

A persuasive argument can be made that the

last of the ten factors to be discussed here should be placed no lower than second or third on this list. This is the geographical orientation of the parish. If the congregation is strongly oriented toward reaching and serving people who live within a half mile or perhaps a mile of the building, it is far less likely to grow in numbers than if it is oriented to reach, attract, and serve people living within a ten- or twenty-mile radius. As the primary point of socialization has moved out of the neighborhood into the place of work (and into the place of education, the place of shopping, the place of recreation) and as people expect high quality responses to their needs, the geographical parish has been rendered obsolete. This also reflects generational differences as younger adults display a greater willingness to drive a long distance to church than do people born before 1930.

This obviously overlaps several of the variables mentioned earlier and that is one reason it is placed tenth.

While this is not offered as a comprehensive list of the variables influencing church growth, it does reflect the judgment of this student of the ecclesiastical scene that for the majority of congregations population growth trends rank no higher than eleventh on the list of variables that will affect the potential for growth.

What Do You Ask?

In those situations where population growth or decline patterns do have considerable relevance, it might be useful to ask three specific questions. The first concerns the change in the social class characteristics of the population. In terms of measurable social class characteristics (income, education, employment) do the newcomers rank higher or lower on that scale than those moving away? Most churches find it relatively easy to grow in numbers and move up the social class scale. It is rare, however, to find a congregation that has been growing in numbers while moving down the social class scale.[1]

A second question to ask is the rate of turnover. In one community eight hundred people moved in during the previous year and nine hundred residents left for a net decrease in the population of one hundred. In a nearby community of the same size during the same year three hundred people moved in, and only two hundred left for a net growth of one hundred. The potential for either numerical growth or numerical decline was greater for the churches in the first community, but most long-established congregations are likely to find the second pattern a more comfortable one. Most churches prefer stability, not mobility, when developing a church-growth strategy.

The third variable that usually is more signficant than the raw figures on population growth or decline is to look at the age and marital status of the newcomers. If during a particular year five hundred residents who represent married couples aged forty and older move away and are replaced by six hundred young never-married adults, the churches in that community are not likely to grow. If, by contrast, six hundred young unmarried residents moved away and are replaced by only two hundred husband-wife couples (four hundred people), all aged forty-five and over, the likelihood of the churches experiencing numerical growth is far greater.

In other words the composition of the changes in the nearby population may be far more significant than simple growth or decline statistics.

What do you believe? Do you believe the quantitative changes are more significant than the factors raised in these three questions? Do you believe the external population growth or decline trends influence the potential for growth in most congregations? Or do you believe the internal factors in congregational stance and priorities may be more influential? Or do you believe other even more decisive factors should be included in ths list? Do you believe the church scene is far more competitive than it was thirty or forty years ago and that people will travel long distances to find the church that is responsive to their needs? Or do you believe that population growth will produce an increase in membership of the churches?

Your answers to these questions not only will determine the questions you ask and the data you gather for your decision-making processes, but will also influence the formulation of goals and the priorities in allocating resources in your congregation.

NOTE

1. Those interested in examining the historical impact of social class on churches, see Wayne Meeks, *The First Urban Christians* (New Haven: Yale University Press, 1983).

Do Fewer People Need More Room?

"We want to organize a new congregation out on the west side and we've narrowed our search down to three sites," explained the denominational official as he unrolled some maps and began a conversation with a city planner one Tuesday afternoon in 1952. "One choice is to purchase four residential lots right next to the proposed elementary school near the center of this subdivision. That would give us a site with a hundred feet of frontage and 260 feet of depth. A second possibility is a one-acre parcel in a retail district at the corner of Higgins Road and Fairmont Avenue. The third is a 300′ × 150′ site at this T intersection where Oak Street deadends at Highland Avenue. If you were in my shoes, which would you buy?"

After perhaps thirty or forty seconds of reflection, the planner replied, "If I were you, I wouldn't buy any of them. The first is a little over a half acre in size and the other two are about an acre each. I think you need a minimum of two acres, and if I were you, I would try to find a three-acre parcel. With two acres you can use one acre for your building and setbacks and use the other acre for parking, walks, landscaping, and your driveway."

"Do you know what that would cost?" objected the denominational official.

"Yep, out where you're looking, three acres of raw land would cost you between $3,000 and $4,500. If you buy improved land with the streets, sewer, and water in, you'll probably have to pay $6,000 to $8,000 an acre."

Despite that advice, the decision was made to purchase the four lots next to the elementary school in the middle of that subdivision. A congregation was started that summer, the first building was completed in 1955, the congregation peaked with 115 at worship in 1963, and dropped to 55 during a four-year pastorate in the late 1960s that was a disastrous mismatch between parishioners and pastor. After several years of ups and down, a bi-vocational minister, who works a full week as a physicist in a research laboratory, arrived in 1979, and the congregation has stabilized with an average attendance of 85 at Sunday morning worship.

The young couples with three or four children per family have been replaced by empty nesters. The elementary school was closed in 1981, the building was converted into professional offices, and one-half of the residents of that neighborhood now are past sixty years of age. Several of the carports have been enclosed, but most have been replaced by two-car garages. Many of the three-bedroom ranch homes have been remodeled, and one of the bedrooms has been turned into a family room. In several cases the owner has knocked out the wall separating the two smaller bedrooms and remodeled that space into one large bedroom with a walk-in closet at one end, and a full bath has been added at the other end.

What had been designed as a residence for five or six people in 1952 is now a comfortable, but slightly crowded when company comes, home for a mature couple. Several of the couples living here spend one or two winter months in their mobile home in the Sunbelt. Several other homes in this subdivision are now occupied by a widowed mother, her divorced daughter, and one or two grandchildren.

This brief case study from a midwestern city that reported 85,000 residents in the 1950 census could be duplicated in scores of communities. Among the other points it illustrates are (a) the aging of the American population, (b) the increasing number of people retiring before their sixtieth birthday and retaining a home in the North while spending the winter months in the Sunbelt, (c) the impact on the public school systems of the "birth dearth" of the 1970s, (d) the increase in the number of one-generation households, (e) the growing number of small churches that have been priced out of the preacher market and no longer can afford their own full-time resident minister, and (f) the expanding market for plumbing fixtures and other materials needed for remodeling older houses.

The reason for telling that story here, however, is to illustrate the point that today more space is needed to accommodate fewer people than was true thirty-five years ago. The thesis of this chapter is that one of the subtle changes of the past several decades has been the rising expectations of people for more space. This can be illustrated by a score of examples.

1. The long-established congregation, which had averaged between eighty-five and a hundred at Sunday morning worship for over a half century, but has dropped in recent years to an average of seventy to seventy-five, felt constrained to construct an addition to their white frame building a few years ago. The addition includes an up-to-date kitchen, a small fellowship hall, two rest rooms, an office for the minister, and two Sunday school classrooms. Now that it has been completed and been used for several years, the two most frequently heard reflections are, "How in the world did we get along without it before?" and "You know, I said at the time we should have built it bigger, and I think now nearly everyone agrees with me."

2. Today, unless local or economic conditions make this impossible, most experts in new church development agree the site for a new church should be a minimum of seven to ten acres. As a general rule, a congregation averaging approximately a hundred at worship needs two acres of land, and an additional acre is needed for each additional one hundred people at worship. Thus the new mission that is expected to grow to nine hundred at worship on Sunday morning probably will need a ten-acre site.

In those municipalities with stringent requirements for off-street parking, setbacks, storm water retention basins, traffic flow, and preservation of existing trees, two acres will be needed for every one hundred people at worship. If that congregation also plans to operate a Christian Day School or a child care center or a Bible college or a retirement village or a nursing home, even two acres per one hundred people at worship may be insufficient.

3. The closets in the bedrooms of single-family homes today usually have three or four times as many cubic feet of space as the closets in the houses constructed in 1950.

4. The space for the storage of automobiles in private homes doubled or tripled between 1955 and 1990.

5. The ratio of bathrooms to bedrooms has doubled or tripled since 1950.

6. The typical kitchen in the home constructed in the 1980s was double or triple the size of the kitchen in homes constructed in the 1950s.

7. The number of square feet of floor space per pupil in the elementary school constructed in 1950 was quadruple the average for elementary school buildings constructed in 1900 and tripled again for elementary schools constructed in 1985.

8. The number of square feet of floor space per patient for hospitals constructed today is quadruple the floor space per patient for hospitals built in 1935.

9. The number of vehicles required to bring 100 people to church today is at least 50 percent greater than the number of cars required to bring 100 people to church in 1955.

10. The number of people who will be *comfortably* seated in twelve-foot long pews today is only four or five compared to six in 1950.

11. The number of square feet of office space needed for the program staff in the fifteen-hundred-member church today is triple or quadruple the space required in 1950.

An intensive study of more than 500 rural churches in Missouri in 1952 found that only 12 percent provided an office for the minister and only one-fourth included a kitchen in the church. When that study was replicated 30 years later, two-thirds of all churches included a kitchen, and the proportion providing an office for the minister had nearly quadrupled to 42 percent.[1]

12. The ideal narthex of today should be at least three or four times the size of what was considered to be acceptable in 1955.

In 1955 it was widely assumed, although rarely true, that every church should serve a geographically defined community and thus the members would see one another frequently during the week. Today it is far less common for members to encounter one another except at church. Therefore a larger narthex is needed to reinforce social ties, to welcome first-time visitors, to encourage lingering, and to facilitate finding a name tag before entering the sanctuary or auditorium.

13. In 1935, the typical residential lot for a single-family house was 30, 33, or 40 feet wide. Today most new single-family homes are constructed on lots that are at least 60 feet wide, despite a sharp decrease in the number of people who probably will be living in that house. Many

municipalities now require at least 70 feet of frontage in new subdivisions.

In 1948, the typical "starter home" for the young couple who were buying their first house was a one-story structure 24 feet wide and 32 feet long, for the total of 768 square feet, with two bedrooms. Some were only 28 feet long. Today, tens of thousands of young couples buying their first home limit their search to houses containing at least 1,200 to 1,500 square feet of space, and many buy a house with over 2,000 square feet of interior space.

14. In 1985 the average farm in the United States contained 445 acres, more than double the average farm size of 216 acres in 1950.

15. The number of one-person households in the United States tripled from 6.9 million in 1960 to over 21 million in 1987.

16. The average number of persons per household in the United States has dropped from 5.79 in 1790 to 4.93 in 1890 to 3.33 in 1960 to 2.66 in 1988.

17. The population density of the older American central cities has dropped sharply since 1945, but still is higher than for the newer cities. In 1980, for example, the population density of Boston was nearly 12,000 persons per square mile, Chicago was over 13,000 persons per square mile, Cleveland was 7,300 (one-half the population density of 1945), Detroit was 8,900, the borough of Manhattan was 64,000, Philadelphia was 12,400, and Pittsburgh was 7,600.

By contrast, in 1980 the population density of Denver was 4,500 persons per square mile, Dallas 2,700, Houston 2,900, Oklahoma City 700,

Orlando 3,300, Atlanta 3,300, Little Rock 2,000, Mobile 1,600, Birmingham 2,900, Honolulu 4,200, San Jose 4,000, Los Angeles 6,400, Phoenix 2,400, Tucson 3,300, Des Moines 2,900, Wichita 2,800, Las Vegas 3,000, Albuquerque 3,500, and Lincoln 2,900. In the newer suburban cities the population density usually is under 3,000 persons per square mile.

18. The size of the chancel in the typical new Protestant building is at least double what was seen as the appropriate size in 1955.

19. The choir loft designed for fifty people in 1950 now feels crowded when the choir exceeds forty voices.

20. The number of square feet of office space required to house the staff of the regional judicatory of your denomination today is at least double or triple what it was in 1950.

The common thread running through these examples is that each generation feels a need for more space. Do you believe that? If you do, it may be useful to look at a few of the implications.

What Are the Implications?

For local church leaders, perhaps the most obvious implication is that the congregation that expects to grow older and smaller together can ignore everything written here. By contrast, however, the congregation that is seriously and actively interested in reaching and serving the generations born after the end of World War II can anticipate that success will be accompanied by a demand for more space. For many long-established urban churches, the first demand will be for additional off-street parking. As was pointed out earlier, today it requires three or four vehicles to bring the same number of people to church as came in two cars in 1952.

For many churches, the least pressing demands will be more space for people to gather for the corporate worship of God. The general drift in the direction of offering multiple worship services on the weekend has offset much of that pressure. The room the architect in 1952 claimed would accommodate 250 for worship today conveys the impression it is filled when 200 people gather, but the expansion of the schedule to add an early worship service has relieved most of that pressure. With perhaps 100 people at the early hour and 150 at the second service, there still is room for growth.

The most highly visible demand for more space can be seen in those congregations that were averaging 300 to 700 at Sunday morning worship and recently began to attract huge numbers of people born after 1940. Within a few years, literally scores of these congregations tripled or quadrupled in size. A few found themselves with eight or ten times as many people as had gathered for worship a decade earlier. Many constructed an addition or two or three, but eventually were forced to build a new meetinghouse at a new and far larger site. In the 1950s many central city congregations relocated to the suburbs in an effort to follow the migration of their members. Today the number-one reason for relocation, and this includes a growing number of suburban congregations founded after World War II, is the need for more space.

A second implication is, as was pointed out earlier, the need for a larger and more attractive narthex to facilitate fellowship.

Overlapping that is the need for a large fellowship hall that can seat one-half of the members, or more, at a meal.

Sometimes these two needs are met by designing a very large room that serves as both the narthex and as a general meeting room on other occasions. In a growing number of very large congregations that huge room is the meeting place for the pastor's class held during the Sunday school hour that attracts several hundred people week after week.[1] That big room can be a valuable tool in expanding the number of entry points for potential new members.

Fourth, recent years have brought a growing demand for serious, continuing adult Bible study. This has created a need for more attractive and comfortable rooms that can accommodate thirty-five to forty adults.

In addition, the erosion of denominational loyalties has resulted in the need for a better system for the assimilation of new members. The large group events held in a big fellowship hall can be a significant component of that system. The disappearance of the geographical parish means that many members rarely see one another outside church, so those adult study groups and those large group events in the fellowship hall are means of increasing the opportunities for new members to meet and make new friends from among the members.

Once upon a time the meeting place for Christian churches was designed with the sanctuary as the focal point. This reinforced the centrality of Word and Sacrament. Today the first-time visitor to many large congregations meeting in a new building may have to search for the proper entrance to the sanctuary. It may be much easier to find the parking lot, the fellowship hall, or that large educational wing. This change is partly the result of this growing demand for more space and partly due to the disappearance of the Sunday evening worship service and the Wednesday evening prayer meeting from the weekly schedule of many old-line Protestant churches. The sanctuary no longer is the focal point for congregational life and fellowship. This has reinforced that demand for more and better space for adult classes and for large group events as well as for more off-street parking.

The Generational Gap

For many congregations, the most complex dimension of this demand for more space arises when a group of new and younger members suggests relocating to a larger site and constructing a new building. This often is resisted by older longtime members who do not agree that the need for more space is so urgent and who are reluctant to leave this sacred place that houses so many dear memories. The issue is further complicated by (a) the fact that the votes for relocation may be coming from younger members, but most leaders realize a large share of the cost will be paid by older members, and (b) an unspoken recognition that while the control today may be in the hands of the older longtime members, the future rests largely with the generations born after 1945.

Space for Staff

From a ministerial perspective, one of the most difficult issues arises from the fact that the congregation averaging 300 at worship today almost always will have a larger program staff than the congregation that averaged 300 at worship in 1950. If the building was designed in 1923 or 1950, it almost certainly was planned to house a smaller program staff than is needed today. Where will the offices for the new staff be located? In a classroom? Upstairs in the re-modeled broom closet? Whatever the answer is, it often is one that undercuts internal communication among the staff.

Weekday Versus Sunday

From the perspective of many of the members born before 1930, the most extravagant response to this issue of space and turf can be found in the growing number of congregations that have abandoned the "multiple use of space" dream that was so widely endorsed in the 1960s. Instead of the Sunday school classes for young children meeting in the same rooms used by the weekday nursery school, each has its own wing in the building. Instead of the director of Christian education having an office in a room that also was used by a class on Sunday morning, that staff member now has a private office. The dream of having one large room serve as a sanctuary with movable chairs for worship and also as a fellowship hall has been replaced by the dream for a new sanctuary with pews.

The dream of the multiple use of space was widely shared among people born before 1940, but has relatively few supporters among those born after 1950. Privacy and demand for "my own space" has supplanted that emphasis on economy.

What's Ahead?

While many old-timers remain convinced the pendulum will swing back and that the younger members, when they mature, will affirm the values of economy and be willing to be crowded in order to save money, there is little evidence to support that hope.

The basic trend lines indicate that congregations seeking to reach and serve a younger generation of members will have to provide and maintain more space to accommodate the same number of people. That costs money, but no one ever promised that change would come without costs. One of these costs in congregations where the membership is growing younger is the demand for more space and for better quality space. The younger generations seek more space than older generations feel is either necessary or feasible.

What do you believe the future will bring? A continued demand for more space? Or a return to the values of the 1950s and 1960s when the goals of economy and efficiency dominated the policy-making discussions about the need for more space? Your answer will influence your decisions.

NOTE

1. For a description of this type of adult Sunday school class, see Lyle E. Schaller, *The Senior Minister* (Nashville: Abingdon Press, 1988), pp. 146-48.

Is the Learning Curve Real?

What makes the great chess players so good? Nobel Laureate Herbert Simon studied dozens of great chess players and discovered most of them had memorized between 25,000 and 50,000 patterns they could recognize when that pattern appeared on the chessboard. That enabled these master chess players to make the appropriate next move. It also makes it possible for some to participate in games with several different opponents simultaneously. These chess players reported that it required a minimum of ten years of concentrated effort to memorize that many patterns.

The cabinet maker with twenty years of experience can turn out better cabinets faster than can the apprentice. Most patients going into the operating room feel more comfortable if they know the surgeon has performed that same operation successfully hundreds of times before. Few seek out the surgeon who admits, "I've never performed that operation before, but I would like to learn, and I promise I'll be careful."

Very few baseball players became stars in the major leagues without at least three or four years of experience in the minors. The fourth-grade teacher with seven years of classroom experience usually can be expected to be a more effective teacher than the person who graduated from a school of education last June.

These examples illustrate a concept called the learning curve. The third automobile to come off the new assembly line is more likely to have several defects than the seventy-thousandth car to be assembled in that factory.

Do you believe the learning curve is an important factor in the parish ministry? Perhaps the best way to test your response to this concept is to raise five questions about what you believe about the parish ministry.

1. How long should the minister, who just graduated from seminary, plan to stay in that first pastorate when that is a two-hundred-member rural congregation?

If you focus on the career path of that minister, you might suggest, "You really cannot afford to spend more then three or four years in that first small parish unless you expect to specialize in serving small rural churches." If that recent seminary graduate had grown up in a large suburban church, attended a huge state university, and graduated from an urban seminary, you might add, "You can learn all you'll ever need to know about both rural America and the small church in four years. By the middle of that fourth year you will have passed the peak of your learning curve for that type of experience, and you should think about moving on to a new and more challenging experience."

If, however, the life and ministry of that small rural parish is your primary concern, you might offer this advice, "Given your urban background and that network of kinfolk and friendship ties that often are at the heart of the small rural church, you probably will need at least five years to get to know that many people in sufficient depth that you will understand their religious needs and that they will trust you. Along about the sixth or seventh year you may have the degree of trust necessary to introduce some ideas that will strengthen, reinforce, and expand the ministry of that congregation. If you reach the peak of the learning curve in year five and take another six or seven years to build on that foundation, you should be able to make a lasting difference in the lives of those people and in the ministry and outreach of that congregation."

Do you believe when a pastor reaches the peak of the learning curve that represents the appropriate time to move to another parish?

Or do you believe that the most productive years of a pastorate cannot begin until the peak of that learning curve has been reached?

Those two questions should be on the agendas of both pastor and of those responsible for ministerial placement!

2. What should be the tenure of the associate pastor?

Should this position be seen as the post-seminary apprentice for someone who seeks a couple of years' experience in a large congregation under the tutelage of a master senior minister before "going out on my own"? Or should that position be reserved for seminary graduates who are still wrestling with their call and are not yet committed to the parish ministry? Or should this role be filled by an experienced pastor in those pre-retirement years?

In each of these three alternatives a persuasive case can be made for a pastorate of three to five years.

Or do you believe this should be seen as a highly specialized role demanding a far above average level of competence, creativity, pastoral ability, humility, productivity, managerial skills, and versatility?

If you choose this definition of the role of the associate pastor in the large church, a strong case can be made for a twenty-to-thirty-year tenure for an associate minister. The combination of the size, complexity, high turnover, and broad program means it may be at least twenty years before the learning curve of that associate minister begins to flatten out.

3. What do you believe is the appropriate tenure for the senior minister of a large and numerically growing congregation?

Do you believe the typical senior minister can be expected to learn and correctly remember the names of a thousand or more members, to build a staff team, to fully understand the unique culture of that complex parish, to develop meaningful relationships with several hundred people, and to perfect the leadership skills necessary for that particular parish in two or three years?

Or do you believe the learning curve for the effective senior minister resembles a staircase that keeps climbing forever and ever? Occasionally that pastor may rest on one step for several weeks and conclude, "I believe I finally fully understand this parish." A few months later, however, that senior minister is struck by a startling insight that may create the reaction, "How in the world did I survive this long here without knowing that?"

If you believe the learning curve for the good senior minister keeps climbing forever, you probably will favor long pastorates. You also may agree that when a senior minister becomes convinced that spiraling learning curve has become a plateau and the performance reflects that, the time has come for that senior minister to move.

4. What do you believe about limiting the tenure of denominational officers and lay volunteers in the church?

In a wonderful comic record, *2000 and One Years with Carl Reiner and Mel Brooks*, produced in 1973, the 2000-year-old man is asked about the means of transportation twenty centuries earlier. The 2000-year-old man replied, "Mostly fear . . . fear was the means of propulsion."

A parallel question could be, What is the primary motivation for limiting the tenure of presidents, governors, bishops, pastors, Sunday school superintendents, trustees, and members of committees?

A few may respond, "We need to encourage turnover in order to give more people the opportunity to serve." The historical record, however, is clear that the number-one reason has been fear. This includes fear of tyrannical leadership, fear that leader may gain an excessive amount of power, and the fear represented by Lord Acton's famous comment in his letter of April 5, 1887, to Bishop Mandell, "Power tends to corrupt and absolute power corrupts absolutely."

The number-one argument *against* limited tenure is the learning curve. One widely discussed example is the six-year limitation in office for a district superintendent in The United Methodist Church. The main source of the pressure for retaining that rule is the fear that with unlimited tenure the superintendent could acquire excessive power.

The other side of that argument is represented by those who contend, "It takes two or three years to learn the job and in the last year the superintendent is a lame duck, so that means only a couple of years of effective service." That argument assumes the learning curve is only two or three years before peaking. That may understate the complexity of the job, especially if the district includes opportunities for new church development, the relocation of churches from obsolete or inadequate sites, several inner-city congregations, a couple of very large multiple-staff churches, a few ethnic minority congregations, and several rural parishes. To expect someone to develop a reasonable level of competence in all of those specialties in two or three or four years is somewhere between optimism and utter naïveté. While it is impossible to prove a simple cause-and-effect relationship, it is not irrelevant to note that the limited tenure of district superintendents has been accompanied by the closing of an average of more than four hundred churches annually for the past hundred years in the denominations now represented by The United Methodist Church.

Between January 1, 1974, and December 31, 1986, this limitation on tenure has been accompanied by (a) a reduction in the average size of The United Methodist congregation, (b) the closing of 2,000 congregations; (c) an increase from 9,711 congregations averaging under 35 at worship in 1974 to 10,355 in 1986—despite that closing of 2,000 churches; (d) a decrease of 777 in the number of congregations averaging 100 or more at worship; (e) a decrease of 120,000 in average worship attendance; and (f) a drop of 450,000 in the average attendance in Sunday church school. Those figures suggest that today the length of the learning curve for a new district superintendent may be more than two or three years before it flattens out.

If the focus is changed to the rotation of officers and committee members in the local church, the issue can be described as a tradeoff. Which side of the tradeoff do you prefer? Do you prefer to encourage short tenure to minimize "burnout," to give fresh opportunities to that passing parade of new members, to reduce the risk that someone will accumulate excessive power, to encourage bringing new perspectives into those standing committees, to give more people a chance to serve, to continue the flow of "new blood" into policy-making groups, and to encourage broad-based participation?

Or do you believe the learning curve also applies to local church offices and that three to five years are required to build up the level of competence of volunteers? Do you believe performance is a higher value in building that team of lay volunteers than is broad-based participation?

Do you believe that it is easier to master the responsibilities that go with serving as a trustee or a member of the finance committee than it is to master the skills necessary to be an effective member of the Christian education committee or the evangelism commission or the task force on hunger or the worship committee? If you do, you may want to encourage longer tenure for the members of the program committees and shorter terms of office for those serving on administrative committees. Applying the same rules on rotation of office to all committees is one means of increasing the probability that the committees responsible for real estate and finances will dominate the decision-making processes.

Why? Because the committees with the most highly skilled leadership will tend to have greater influence in setting congregational priorities. Many laypeople bring a high level of competence in finance and real estate with them when asked to serve on those committees. Thus the learning curve may be relatively short. Relatively few of the laity bring an equivalent level of skill when asked to serve on an evangelism or missions or worship committee and thus the learning curve may be much longer. To equalize the influence will require longer tenure for members of those ministry committees.

5. What should be the tenure of Sunday school teachers?

If you are convinced the central problem is the difficulty in enlisting volunteers to teach in the Sunday school, you may reply, "Six weeks," or "Three months." Frequently it is easier to enlist people for a short-term responsibility than for a long-term assignment.

If, however, you are convinced (a) the learning curve also applies to teaching in the Sunday school, (b) the relationships between the teacher and the members of that class are at least as critical as the content being studied, (c) the pedagogical methods appropriate for teaching a class of six-year-olds are not the same as those needed in a class of sixteen-year-olds or thirty-nine-year-olds, (d) pedagogical skills can be taught, but rarely can be learned and perfected in a few months, and (e) there is value in the continuity of relationships and the design of the class, you may favor far longer tenure for your Sunday school teachers.

One version is the team of three teachers who are asked to teach the fifth- and sixth-grade class this next year. The following year they teach the sixth- and seventh-grade class, and the third year that same team teaches the seventh- and eighth-grade class. This system resembles the one in which the Bethany Class, now composed of people in their late forties and early fifties, has enjoyed the leadership of the same teacher ever since it was organized as a class for newlyweds twenty-six years ago.

What do you believe about the relevance of the learning curve to the parish ministry? Your answer will influence the decisions you make on scores of subjects. One of these, which frequently is over-looked, is the difference between bringing together a group of strangers to work together and the productivity of a group of people who have several years of experience as members of that team.

Linkages and Networks

"One of the major accomplishments for the feminist movement is that it has encouraged women to create networks that enable us to help one another," declared a thirty-five-year-old mother of two who no longer was employed outside the home. "Even though I quit my job four years ago to stay home with my children, I'm on the phone several times a day. This morning, for example, I received a telephone call from a friend at church asking if I thought Sally Thompson, who is a mutual friend, would be interested in a new position that is being created in her husband's law firm. We've both known Sally for several years, and my friend immediately thought of Sally when her husband mentioned they were creating this new position. It was a similar network of friends that helped Jack and me find this apartment two years ago."

* * *

"I think the university would be lucky if you would take it, but do you want to leave here?" questioned a close friend of a United Methodist minister who had been invited to become dean of the chapel at a large church-related university in another part of the country. "You realize if you leave this conference, you'll be leaving all your close friends behind. That conference has its own network and there you'll be an outsider for several years."

* * *

"I wouldn't even know whom to call in Louisville," declared the Presbyterian minister in Louisiana who had been advised by a friend to seek help from the national staff for a particular problem. "In the old PCUS I was personally acquainted with at least half of the staff in Atlanta and with one or two telephone calls I could have found the help I need. I guess I never realized that one of the price tags on reuniting the Northern and Southern Presbyterians would be the destruction of those linkages."

The destruction of the linkages and networks that enabled a denominational structure to be sensitive and responsive to the needs of both congregations and people is a price tag on denominational mergers that seldom is fully comprehended until after the fact.[1]

* * *

Four months after his arrival as the pastor of the two-hundred-seventy-member Maple Glen Church, the Reverend Dale Bowman discovered Marie Brown's husband, Steve, had been Clara Green's first husband. Steve and Clara had been divorced twenty-five years earlier, and subsequently Steve had married Marie. The following year Clara had married Homer Wentworth. Today Marie, Steve, Clara, and Homer are all active members of the Maple Glen Church. "If someone had told me that when I first arrived, I could have saved myself some embarrassment!" thought the minister as he drove away from what had turned out to be a disastrous pastoral call on Homer and Clara Wentworth.

* * *

"Everyone told me how lucky I was to receive the call to this parish," reflected Sue Hanson, the new pastor at Trinity Lutheran Church. "The bishop and everyone who knew my predecessor told me he was a superb administrator and this was an exceptionally well organized parish. Well, they were right. It was very well organized, but that organizational structure had been built around the gifts, skills, personality, and twenty-two-year tenure of my predecessor. When he left to take a call to a church in New Mexico, he also took most of the glue that held that structure together. I'm a different person with a different set of gifts and skills than he had. Please understand, I'm not blaming him; he did what he was comfortable doing. However, what everyone described as a well-organized parish turned out, from my perspective, to be a set of networks and linkages with him at the hub of the network. He was the link that tied one part of the structure into the rest of the system. One of my top priorities is to build a new organizational structure that I'm comfortable with and that will serve this parish."

How long do you believe it will take Pastor Hanson to build a new system of networks and linkages in that parish? Do you agree that should be a high priority for her? Or, to place it in more general terms, do you believe networks and linkages are important? Do you believe they reflect an organizational structure that can be dia-grammed on a sheet of paper and that is composed of interchangeable parts? If you do, you may conclude the learning curve for a newcomer to that organizational structure should be relatively brief.

Or, do you believe that the skills, gifts, experi-ences, personality, age, education, gender, race, ethnic background, theological stance, and the friendship (and kinship) ties of each person in that organizational structure have a great influence on how that system functions? If you agree that may be a closer representation of reality, you may agree the learning curve also applies to both the creation of networks and linkages and also to how long it may take a newcomer to become a productive participant in that system.

In general terms, those who believe (a) the learning curve is real and (b) the greater the complexity of that organization, the longer the period of time before the learning curve begins to flatten out, also favor long tenure. Those who favor short tenure tend not to believe in the learning curve. What do you believe?

NOTE

1. Douglas W. Johnson and Alan K. Waltz, *Facts and Possibilities* (Nashville: Abingdon Press, 1987).

Does Two Plus Two Equal Eight?

"Alan, I've got a great idea for you to think about," declared Bob Baxter as he and his wife, Betty, gathered for their monthly dinner with Alan and Ellen Cole. Bob and Alan had been classmates in college, and Betty and Bob had introduced Alan and Ellen to each other thirty-four years earlier. Each couple had been a part of the other's wedding party, and they had continued to be extremely close friends through the years. Betty and Ellen had helped work their husbands' way through theological seminary; Bob and Alan had been in the same graduating class twenty-nine years earlier. Both had preferred to pastor small churches, and each was now in his fifth pastorate.

For nearly fifteen years they had been several hundred miles apart, but the two families often vacationed together. Six years ago Bob had come to serve the thirty-nine-year-old Ridgecrest Church in the northwest quadrant of the city where both couples now lived. This congregation averages about 115 at Sunday morning worship.

Two years after he arrived, Bob learned the pastor of Central Church was planning to take early retirement.

Central Church had been founded in 1927 and subsequently had helped sponsor the new Ridgecrest mission. At its peak, in the mid-1950s, Central Church had averaged well over 400 at Sunday morning worship, but in recent years that part of the city had been changing from residential and retail to light industrial uses. When he heard of the future vacancy, Bob urged his old friend, Alan, that he was just exactly the minister Central Church needed, and several months later Alan turned out to be the one chosen for Central Church.

After he arrived, Alan concluded the potential was not what he had been led to believe it was, but he excelled in one-to-one relationships with people, and that soon won him broad support from what had become, for the most part, a congregation of mature adults that averaged a little over a hundred at worship. A big fringe benefit was the move. The Baxters now lived less than two miles from the Coles.

The youngest of the Coles' four children was twenty-one, and the youngest of the three Baxter children was now twenty-two. Several years earlier, after being full-time homemakers for nearly two decades, both Ellen and Betty had reentered the labor force. Ellen is the vice president for public relations in a local bank, and Betty has just been promoted to director of nursing in the largest hospital in the city.

On this particular evening the Coles were hosts

to the Baxters for their Saturday dinner.

"I've been waiting two weeks to spring this on you," continued Bob as he looked at Alan. "We should merge Central Church with Ridgecrest! We could take the money the Central Church property would bring on the market and use it toward building the sanctuary called for in our master plan. We've been worshiping in what originally was intended to be the fellowship hall. We could build a sanctuary that would seat 300 or more and right off we could be a congregation averaging 220 or more at worship."

"That's a great idea!" exclaimed Alan. "After all, our church keeps on bragging about helping sponsor Ridgecrest, and I think, if they had time to talk themselves into it, our people would go for it. At least half of them now live closer to Ridgecrest than to Central. With you and me working together, in five years we could be averaging 330 at worship."

"Why settle for that?" challenged Bob. "Why not build a sanctuary big enough to accommodate 400 or 500 at worship? I'll bet we could get a half million for your property and that would give us a great start on a building fund."

"When should we spring it on our people?" asked Alan who was even more excited with the possibilities than Bob. "I think this will be real easy to sell to our people."

"Honey, what do you think of this?" inquired an enthusiastic Alan as he turned to Ellen.

"It's great to see you two so excited," replied Ellen, "but I don't think either one of you is wired for two-twenty. You've each spent nearly thirty years pastoring small churches. That's what you know best, that's what you love to do, that's where your gifts are, and that's where you belong. If you merge these two congregations, I think you'll end up with one small congregation that can't afford two ministers. If you use the money from the sale of the Central property to build a new sanctuary that can seat 400, I'm afraid that by the time it's finished, it'll turn out to be three-quarters empty on Sunday morning. You're trying to produce a football team by merging two basketball teams."

Shocked into momentary silence by that unexpected bucket of ice cold water from Ellen, Bob Baxter finally looked at his wife and asked, "Well, Betty, what do you think?"

"Well, when you first brought this up a week ago, I began to get excited over it, but the more I think about it, the more I'm convinced Ellen is right," commented Betty rather slowly. "If this is part of a mid-life crisis you're going through, and you really feel a deep need to prove your virility, I think it might be better if you bought that little two-passenger sports car you've been looking at for the past three or four months. I have to agree with Ellen. Both of you guys are small-church ministers. That's what you do best, and that's what I think you should keep on doing."

"Thanks, Betty, for the support," interrupted Ellen. "I'm afraid merging these two churches with the idea that you two would constitute a co-pastorate might turn out to be an effective means of terminating a beautiful friendship. Just because you two are so highly compatible personally doesn't mean you would be compatible professionally."

What Happens?

An examination of hundreds of mergers of local churches suggests Ellen and Betty are right. Merging a congregation that averages 85 at worship with one that averages 80 tends to produce, after a few years, one that averages 85 to 100 at worship. The same pattern tends to prevail when the numbers are 400 and 350 or 35 and 25 or 105 and 115. Two plus two tends to equal two or three, not four. A parallel illustration is the 1957 merger that united the 1.3 million member Congregational Christian Church with the 760,000 member Evangelical and Reformed Church to create the United Church of Christ that, thirty years after the merger, reported slightly under 1.7 million members. A parallel example was the 1958 union of the 2.8 million member Presbyterian Church in the United States of America with the 230,000 member United Presbyterian Church in North America. By 1961 that new denomination had grown to include more than 3.2 million members, but by 1982 the total had dropped to 2.3 million members. A third example is the 1968 merger of the 0.7 million member Evangelical United Brethren with the 10.2 million member Methodist Church to produce a denomination with 9.1 million members two decades later.

Why do so many mergers fail to fulfill the expectations for growth?

One reason for this was identified by Ellen. Her

comment apparently was a takeoff on that ancient joke about the husband who raised the possibility of trading his forty-year-old wife in for two twenty-year-olds. His wife cruelly pointed out that he was not wired for two-twenty voltage. The parallel is that Bob and Alan had spent twenty-nine years perfecting their skills in serving small churches. Neither was prepared to serve far larger congregations. Much of what they had learned and many of the skills they had perfected were entirely appropriate for small churches, but would be counterproductive in a larger church.[1]

What Are the Barriers?

These comments do not mean that every merger is doomed to produce disappointments. The history of both congregational and denominational mergers since 1950, however, suggests that an excessively simplistic approach to the merger of two congregations is likely to demonstrate that two plus two does not automatically equal four.

The most powerful factor is what can be called congregational culture or what others have identified as a behavior setting.[2] Small churches usually display a distinctive congregational culture that includes, among many other characteristics: (1) a high value on one-to-one relationships, (2) a heavy dependence on kinship and friendship ties as cohesive factors, (3) an above average degree of informality in congregational life, (4) a relatively short-time frame for planning, (5) a limited role for committees, and (6) a modest program.

Thus when the congregation averaging 55 at worship is merged with the one averaging 65 at worship, the overly simplistic, but highly attractive course of action is to think in terms of combining two institutions while retaining the best features of each. A more productive approach would be to plan to create a new, larger, radically different and more complex organizational structure. This means creating the type of congregational culture that will be compatible with a middle-sized congregation averaging well over 100 at worship. Unless that congregational culture is changed, powerful institutional pressures usually will shrink the size of the new merged congregation to approximately the size of the larger of the two predecessor bodies. One component of that new culture should be a continuing effort to create the new linkages and the new networks that can replace those disrupted by the merger.

Overlapping the conflicts and limitations that can be traced back to the congregational culture are other barriers that come to light repeatedly in the postmortems of congregational mergers. The most divisive is when two congregations coming from sharply different positions on biblical interpretations and theology seek to merge. A second is when a proposal is made to merge the small and theologically conservative congregation meeting in a building in the open country with a larger and theologically more liberal church in town. The small church sacrifices its distinctive role, its identity, its familiar meeting place, and the power of the relationships that held that group of a dozen to a score of families together. A third is when substantial ethnic or nationality differences exist. One example was the decision by some Anglo leaders to merge a Puerto Rican church with a Cuban church on the assumption both were Hispanic. A fourth is to attempt to merge across social class lines. A fifth common barrier can be seen in the efforts to merge a voluntary association church with a high-demand congregation. (See chapter 1.)

A sixth type of barrier also can be seen in denominational mergers when one group was led by several leaders with a high level of skills in ecclesiastical politics and the leadership of the partner had a much lower level of political skill. A seventh barrier, which is really part of that congregational culture, is when the congregation that is organized largely around a religious belief system seeks to merge with a congregation in which the magnetic personality of the pastor or the inherited power of one or two families or the kinship ties or a highly valued nationality or language heritage or the attachment to the cemetery represent most of the glue that holds that collection of people together.

Some of these barriers to successful mergers can be identified in both denominational and congregational efforts to make two plus two equal four.

If and when two small congregations unite as part of a long-term strategy to create a middle-sized or large church, one of four patterns usually will emerge from that effort.

1. No one makes any effort to alter the

congregational culture and the new merged church soon shrinks to approximately the size of the larger of the two former congregations.[3]

2. The inspiring leadership ability of the minister overrides the power of the congregational culture and the new merged church creates a new culture appropriate to a larger number of people that also is attractive to newcomers and facilitates the assimilation of new people who help reinforce a new style of congregational life, a set of new traditions, an expansion of the program and the addition of more program staff, and the newly merged church continues to grow in numbers. As it grows, members from each of the predecessor congregations are joined by new members in creating that essential web of networks, new linkages, new rallying points, and a new set of small face-to-face groups.

3. The excitement, enthusiasm, momentum, and goal-driven orientation that is a part of pioneering the creation of that new merged church sustains that larger size for a few years. Within four or five years, however, one or both of the ministers who encouraged the merger depart and/or the informal pressures to recreate a small church atmosphere and/or the predictable tendency to cut back on schedule, program, staff, finances, or outreach and/or the dominance of a few leaders from one of the predecessor congregations combine to produce a gradual erosion of the numbers. This numerical decline is facilitated by the erosion of the old networks and the failure to create new face-to-face groups. Before long the new church is about the size of the larger of the

two congregations that entered into the merger.

4. With the assistance of denominational staff and/or the new minister and/or the influx of new lay leadership, the people who negotiated the merger agreement see the need to create a new congregational culture or behavior setting that is compatible with the larger size of the new merged church and those decisions are implemented.

A simple, but not common, example of this is where the congregation that averages 110 at worship unites with the congregation that once averaged 275 at worship, but has shrunk to an attendance of 140 to 160. The smaller congregation moves in with the larger congregation at its meeting place. Natural and predictable pressures surface either to (1) retain the pastor from the smaller congregation who will carry a large share of the responsibility for visitation and the pastoral care of the mature members and shut-ins or (2) replace that pastor with a semi-retired minister who will carry that part of the work load.

Instead of going down that attractive road, however, the leaders decide to allocate those financial resources for staffing the greatly expanded ministry of music that is appropriate and necessary in a larger congregation.

In other words, instead of staffing to maintain those one-to-one relationships, the decision was made to allocate those resources for expanding program, strengthening the group life, and creating new entry points for newcomers. Consistent and persistent efforts are made to develop a congregational life appropriate to a much larger number of members, the program is enlarged, the schedule is expanded, the time-frame for planning is extended, and new program staff members are added to improve the process of enlisting and assimilating new members. Ten years later the new merged congregation is larger with a higher quality ministry and a greatly expanded financial base than was true the day after the merger was consummated. The records reveal at least two-thirds of the members have joined since the merger.

The first of these four alternatives is far more common than any of the others while the fourth is the rarest.

2 + 3 + 2 Can Equal 9

The best success stories in creating the new congregational culture that should be a part of any merger process tend to come with the three-church merger when (a) the largest of the three congregations accounts for fewer than one-half of the combined membership and the other two congregations are approximately the same size, (b) the decision is made to create a new congregation that will construct a new building at a new location with a new name, (c) a new minister arrives (and perhaps a completely new program staff if the size justifies that) who is comfortable and competent in the role of being the pastor of a middle-sized (or large) congregation, and (d) within a few years at least one-half of the governing board is composed of people who have joined since the merger and who want to be part of a large and numerically growing congregation.

$8 + 1 = 8$

In other words, the success rate among the mergers bringing together three congregations of approximately the same size is far higher than the two church mergers. The mergers least likely to minimize the erosion of congregational loyalties are those in which a small, and often self-identified "dying congregation," is merged into a very large parish. When the 100-member congregation merges with the 800-member parish, it usually does not take long to produce an 800-member church out of that arrangement, but this arrangement may help "save face" for some of the members of the smaller congregation and it is a means of transferring the assets of that small congregation to the larger church rather than have them dispersed by some other process or turned over to the denomination.[4]

Adding Machine or Cookbook or Chef?

Perhaps the best perspective to use in reflecting on congregational mergers, however, is to forget the arithmetical approach and use a different analogy. Instead of contemplating how to merge an 85-member congregation with a 115-member church to produce a 200-member congregation, it may be more useful to think about baking a cherry pie. It is possible to combine a pint of cherries, some flour, and other ingredients to produce a delicious cherry pie.

The secret of that success, however, is not in the ingredients. The key to that superb pie is in the skill of the person who will transform those raw

147

materials into a delicious cherry pie. Likewise, the proposal to merge two, or even three or four congregations, and to create a new and larger church is not in the personalities of the members of the participating congregations or in some magic formula. The critical component is a minister who is an effective transformational leader and possesses the skills, including the essential people skills, necessary to create a new worshiping community with a new congregational culture, a strong future orientation, a new set of operational goals, a new sense of unity and a new approach to winning a new generation of members.

While a cookbook can be useful to the beginning cook, the master chef does not need one. Likewise the most successful mergers are not a product of a manual on how to unite two or three congregations, but rather are the new creation of a transformational leader.

What do you believe about mergers? Do you believe it is advisable, if merger appears to be a logical next step, to encourage the union of two congregations with meeting places close to one another, despite substantial dissimilarities? Or would you prefer to encourage mergers of two highly similar congregations even if their buildings were some distance apart? Which is easier to overcome? Geographical distance or dissimilarities in congregational cultures? Or would you prefer to focus on three-church unions designed to create a new congregation with a new meeting place at a new location under a new name with new leadership? Or are you convinced the crucial component in a successful merger is a transformational leader? Or would you prefer to spend your time and resources on some other subject such as whether or not mergers can produce economies of scale?

NOTES

1. Lyle E. Schaller, *The Senior Minister* (Nashville: Abingdon Press, 1988), pp. 135-37.

2. Seymour B. Sarason, *The Creation of Settings and the Future Societies* (San Francisco: Jossey-Bass Publishers, 1984). Roger G. Barker and Paul V. Gump, *Big School, Small School* (Palo Alto: Stanford University Press, 1964).

3. For a parallel discussion about mergers, in the business world, see Morty Lefkoe, "Why So Many Mergers Fail," *Fortune*, July 20, 1987, pp. 113–14.

4. For a manual on congregational mergers, see Lyle E. Schaller, *Mergers and Unions* (Naperville, Ill.: The Center for Parish Development, 1969).

Is There an Economy of Scale?

"This building is big enough to accommodate four hundred people at worship, and we have plenty of parking," reflected one of the leaders at the Valley View Church which was averaging between one-hundred sixty and one-hundred seventy at worship. "If we could double our attendance, we could reduce our per person costs. Sure, we would have to add a second minister to the staff and maybe hire another secretary, but most of our other costs are fixed. The economies of scale would enable us to have a more efficient operation."

Do you believe that? Do you believe that per unit costs in churches go down as size goes up?

* * *

"Isn't there some way you can change the system to give our small churches a break on apportionments?" pleaded a lay representative to a conference committee charged with revising the formula for the amount of money the conference asked of each congregation. "We have fewer than two hundred members, and we have to support a full-time minister, but on a per member basis the four-hundred-member church only has to raise half as much money to support a minister as we do. The same goes for utilities and insurance and a lot of other fixed costs. Our people are being asked to give and give and give, and some of them are getting sick of it. I don't know the figures right offhand, but I'm sure our small churches contribute a lot more per member than our large congregations."

Do you agree with that analysis and that plea? Do you believe the financial burden is greater on small churches than on large ones?

* * *

Back in the early 1930s it was not difficult to find small town and rural Protestant congregations that averaged thirty to fifty at worship on Sunday morning and were served by a full-time resident minister who did not have any other employment. That minster was almost always a man and rarely was his wife employed outside the home—except when she worked in the garden in the backyard. Gifts of food supplemented the cash salary that seldom was as much as sixty dollars a month. The few dollars received as honoraria for weddings and funerals customarily were given to the wife for household expenses or shoes for the children. Typically these parsonage families lived at or above the average level of living of the rest of the people in that community. Traditionally the local physician did not charge the minister for professional services.

By 1955 the economic base of the ecclesiastical landscape had changed and it was rare to find a congregation averaging fewer than fifty or sixty at worship with its own full-time resident minister. The small churches were being priced out of the preacher market. In some cases the small churches were able to continue with a full-time minister, thanks to (1) one or two generous parishioners, (2) a denominational subsidy, (3) a spouse who was employed outside the home, (4) a pension for the retired military chaplain serving as a pre-retirement vocation, (5) income from an endowment fund, (6) the fact that every member tithed and returned that tithe to the Lord via that church, (7) severe economies in program, or (8) a combination of two or more of these factors.

In other places the "full-time" small town resident minister was able to get by financially by serving another small congregation out in the country.

Today a larger congregation is required to attract, retain, and provide the financial support for a full-time resident minister. Small churches continue to be priced out of the ministerial marketplace.

One response has been for the spouse to seek full-time employment. A second has been an increase in denominational subsidies. A third has been the sharp increase in the number of churches served by a bivocational minister who has a full-time secular job. A fourth has been the closing of hundreds of small congregations every year. A fifth has been the decision by the members of scores of very small congregations to become a lay-led religious community without any paid staff. A sixth was the dream of solving the problem through the merger of small congregations. (This peaked in the late 1960s and early 1970s and no longer has the attraction it once appeared to offer. See chapter 8.)

These and other changes in our society, one of which is the emergence of that rapidly growing number of Protestant congregations averaging over a thousand people at Sunday morning worship, have challenged many of the traditional assumptions about the economics of parish life. Today a larger congregation is needed to provide the financial base for the full-time resident minister than was required sixty years ago.

How large?

That depends on several variables including: (1) the giving level of the members; (2) the availability of a church-owned house, often paid for by previous generations of members, as a residence for the minister; (3) other sources of income for the minister's family (pensions, employment of spouse, savings, assistance from the minister's parents); (4) possible denominational subsidies; (5) income from an endowment fund; (6) income from rental of church property; (7) the salary level for clergy in that denomination; (8) the number and age of the minister's children; (9) the age and marital status of the minister; (10) the proportion of total congregational expenditures the members are willing to allocate to compensation for the pastor; (11) the number and cost of the fringe benefits (pension, health insurance, book allowance, life insurance, housing, expenses for continuing education experiences, reimbursement for Social Security, convention expenses); and (12) unique local circumstances.

If the total cost to a congregation to have a full-time resident pastor comes to $30,000 a year (salary, housing, travel, insurance, pension, and such) and the congregation averages 60 people at worship, that means an average cost of nearly $10 per worshiper every Sunday. That means the husband-wife couple with two children must drop $40 in the offering plate every Sunday they attend just for the costs of a full-time resident pastor. If they attend 40 Sundays a year, that comes to $1,600 annually for that family.

If it is assumed that 50 percent is the maximum proportion of total expenditures in the small church that should be allocated for the minister's support and expenses, that means total expenditures of $60,000 for that congregation that averages 60 at worship. That averages out to $20 per worshiper every week or $3,100 annually for that family of four who attend 40 Sundays a year.

These introductory examples introduce several questions about the economics of parish life.

What Is the Minimum Variable Size?

First, how large should a congregation be today to be able to afford a full-time resident minister? The typical answer is at least 100 to 140 at worship, depending on local variables. That is a substantial change from 60 years ago!

Second, what is the average level of giving by

members in various sized churches? For this purpose the use of the average attendance at worship is a far more reliable and uniform yardstock for comparison purposes than is membership. The criteria for defining membership vary tremendously from congregation to congregation. (See chapter 3.) It also should be recognized many exceptions to these generalizations do exist.

In general, however, congregations averaging under 125 at worship usually reported total member giving in 1988 that averaged out to less than $650 times the average attendance at worship. Thus the congregation averaging 100 at worship usually reported total member giving (exclusive of income from investments, rentals, denominational grants) of less than $65,000. In many small rural congregations total member giving in 1988 averaged out to less than $300 times the worship attendance.

The congregations averaging 350 to 500 at worship usually reported total member giving in 1988 that averaged out to somewhere between $700 and $900 times the average attendance at worship. Thus the congregation averaging 400 at worship might report total member giving of $300,000 to $350,000 for 1988.

Those congregations averaging more than 900 at worship usually found they needed between $1,000 and $2,000 times their average attendance in order to meet all expenses.

In other words, the concept of economy of scale apparently does not apply to larger churches, just as it does not apply to municipal governments, hospitals, and scores of other institutions in our society that provide person-centered services.

Before looking at a few of the reasons behind that generalization, some of the exceptions should be noted. One may be in the costs of building and maintaining a meeting place. It does cost less, for example, to construct and maintain three large classrooms, each one of which can accommodate an adult Sunday school class of five hundred, than to construct and maintain forty classrooms, each one designed to accommodate a class of thirty-five to forty adults. In addition, those three large classrooms may receive more use during the week than will those smaller rooms.

Likewise, it does cost less to build and maintain a room for worship that is filled with two hundred worshipers three times every Sunday morning than it costs to construct and maintain a room that can seat five hundred, but attendance at the one service rarely exceeds two hundred.

Some may argue that it costs no more to prepare a newsletter for eight hundred households than one that is sent to only sixty families, but the printing and postage costs will be higher for the large circulation newsletter than for the small circulation newsletter, and it probably will go out weekly while the small circulation one is mailed only monthly. The per-member costs of internal communication tend to go up as size increases since the grapevine is less reliable.

By and large many of the economies that appear to go with size are either illusions or they are a product of a different approach to ministry (such as a greater emphasis on large groups rather than on small groups) and do not appear until the average attendance at worship passes seven or eight hundred. Frequently these apparent economies of scale are offset by the costs associated with a higher rate of turnover in the membership.

Why do per-person costs go up, rather than down, as size increases? The answer can be compressed in two words—quantity and quality. Typically as the size of the congregation goes up, the members expect a broader program, a greater range of choices, and higher quality. The dream of the economy of scale is offset by the demand for a bigger program and for higher quality in all facets of congregational life from music to the rest rooms to the sermons to the chairs to the ministry of education to parking.

How Much for Staff?

A third question concerns the proportion of total expenditures that should be allocated to the compensation of staff and the costs associated with staff such as travel, pensions, housing, Social Security, continuing education, and insurance.

It is not at all unusual in smaller congregations for this figure to range between 50 and 60 percent. When it exceeds 50 percent, that usually means other obligations are being neglected such as benevolences or program or the maintenance of the property. Many small churches balance the budget by deferring maintenance on the property. Common examples include the decision not to purchase adjacent property for future expansion or to postpone replacing the roof.

In large congregations, that figure typically should not exceed 45 percent of all expenditures and often ranges between 20 and 40 percent in those very large congregations that allocate at least one-third of all expenditures to benevolences and also are financing a big capital improvements program out of current receipts. A fairly common ratio in larger congregations is 30 to 40 percent for staff, 20 percent for program and office expenditures, 25 to 35 percent for missions, and 15 percent for maintenance and capital improvements.

These figures include the total compensation of all staff including secretarial and custodial help plus the cost of maintaining church-owned residences for staff or the payment of housing allowances.

As a general rule the larger the size of the crowd on Sunday morning (a) the higher the level of giving per average attender at worship and (b) the larger the proportion of the total expenditures allocated for benevolences.

A fourth question comes up in larger congregations as the need is recognized to expand the program staff. Should we add another minister? Or should we seek a director of Christian education? Or should we look for a semi-retired pastor to carry a big part of the responsibility for visitation? Or should we expand our music staff?

When measured in terms of costs and productivity, the most expensive staff members often are

the inexperienced full-time ministerial general-
ists. At the other end of the scale the biggest
bargain on the program staff may be the mature
laywoman who is a part-time specialist. Between
these two are the associate pastor with twenty
years' experience who sees this as a special
vocation, the full-time administrative assistant to
the senior minister who combines the roles of
pastor's secretary-church mother-office manager-
business administrator-alter ego of the senior
minister-friend and cheerleader, the full-time lay
program director, and the part-time person
responsible for the assimilation of new members.

As the cost of the total compensation package for
clergy continues to rise, this trend not only is
pricing hundreds of small congregations out of the
preacher market, it also is encouraging that sharp
increase in the ranks of bivocational ministers and
is causing hundreds of large congregations to
replace clergy with lay specialists.

On a cost-per-person-served basis it is not
uncommon for youth ministries to be the most
expensive program in the church. In one congregation, for example, it costs that church $55,000
annually for the total compensation and expenses
of an associate minister who says he spends
one-half of his time working with the junior high
youth group of two dozen people and the senior
high group that includes another two dozen
teenagers who participate with varying degrees
of frequency. That averages out to over $500 per
year per teenager served by those two programs.

What do you believe are the most economically
effective ways to staff the churches?

The Impact of Subsidies

Finally, a few generalizations should be added about denominational subsidies to congregations. The most obvious, objective, and easy-to-measure fact is that this is largely a post-1940 development. Second, the evidence strongly suggests that with rare exceptions denominational subsidies and church growth tend to be mutually exclusive. As a general rule, the longer the congregation has been in existence, the less likely a denominational subsidy to the operating budget will produce numerical growth. (Matching grants for capital expenditures can be a means of encouraging changes that may result in numerical growth.) Third, short-term subsidies of one or two or three years are less likely to be injurious to the spiritual, institutional, and corporate health of a congregation than are long-term subsidies continued for several years. Fourth, the larger the financial subsidy to the operating budget of a new mission, the less likely that new mission will ever reach an average attendance of five hundred or more. Fifth, the higher the income level of the members, the more likely they will be able to make a successful plea for a substantial financial subsidy from denominational headquarters.

What do you believe are the most influential patterns affecting the economic side of parish life? Do any of these generalizations challenge the conventional wisdom followed by your congregation? What do you believe are realistic guidelines?

Protest Movement or Institution Building?

"The founding pastor got into a fight with the leaders of the church he was serving at the time over the issue of racial segregation and in the summer of 1965 he resigned, brought about three dozen of his friends and followers who also strongly supported the Civil Rights Movement with him and started this congregation," explained the thirty-three-year-old minister of the Windsor Heights Church.

"He also switched denominations about the same time because he wanted a more liberal environment. While I never met him, everyone says he was a powerful preacher and he certainly must have been a charismatic leader. By the time he retired a few years ago, this congregation had grown to nearly two hundred members. For the first four years they met in a basement of a bank building. When the congregation that had built this building in the early 1950s decided to relocate because they needed more room, he urged his followers to buy it. We only have a little over an acre of land and so we're beginning to understand why the original owners decided to relocate."

"When did you arrive?" inquired the newest minister in town who was in the process of going around and getting acquainted with the other churches.

"As I said, he retired and died about a year later," came the reply. "He was followed by a minister with impressive credentials, but apparently a complete mismatch for this situation and after fourteen months he left. At that point the denomination intervened and an intentional interim pastor was found who stayed nearly a year and did a superb job of getting things straightened out. I came five years ago."

"What's the picture today?" inquired the visitor. "I arrived less than three months ago, and I'm taking an hour or so every week to get acquainted with one of the other churches around here. Tell me about this church today."

"I really don't know for sure," reflected the pastor. "When I first arrived, I thought I knew what I was getting into, but now I'm not sure. I thought I was coming to a twenty-year-old church that had moved from being a new mission into a congregation that had reached a comfortable plateau and decided not to grow. We have nearly two hundred members. We lost a bunch following the retirement of the founding pastor, but we've replaced most of them. Out of today's members only eleven were here when this congregation met in the bank and six of them are inactive. Nearly half of today's members have joined since I arrived five years ago, but most of our officers and leaders were members before I came."

"What are your greatest points of frustration?" questioned the visitor who had been a newspaper reporter before entering seminary.

"I can give you four answers to that one," came the quick reply. "The most obvious is to try to make one congregation out of two groups of people—the old-timers and the people who've joined since my arrival. When I arrived, I decided the number-one priority would be to help what had been a new mission many years earlier begin to grow again, but that hasn't worked out like I had hoped. As I told you earlier, we've taken in a lot of new members during these past five years, but we've also lost a lot, so our net growth is very modest. That's probably my number-two frustration. My third is getting agreement on what we should do next. The new members want to improve the Sunday school and expand the youth program, but the old-timers want the top priority to be on issue-centered ministries and social action. The fourth point of frustration is that I think we ought to sell this property and relocate to a better spot where we could have sufficient off-street parking and build a new building, but except for a few of the newer members, I can't get anyone interested in that."

"Please pardon me if I sound like I'm giving you the third degree," apologized the visitor, "but I'm curious about what you see is central to life. What do you hold to most dearly in your heart?"

"My faith in Jesus Christ as my personal Savior and my family," was the instant response.

"Maybe you thought I would say this congregation, but sometimes I feel more like a stepchild or a visiting preacher rather than the pastor, especially when I'm with the long-time members."

Now, dear readers, what do you believe is the central dynamic in understanding this situation? Is it the problem of following that long-tenured founding pastor? Or the differences in priorities between the old-timers and the newcomers? Or the inadequacies of a forty-year-old building? Or is the basic issue how to help what has become a mature congregation move off that plateau in size? Or is it the discontinuity in values and goals between the first minister and the current minister?

One response could be "all of the above." A second, and perhaps more useful conceptual framework for diagnostic purposes, would be to go back to the beginnings and seek to understand the dynamics of those early days.

This congregation did not begin simply as a new mission. It resembled far more closely a protest movement led by a magnetic personality who was committed to those causes he summarized under the umbrella of social justice.

At this point it may help to look at the common characteristics of the typical protest movement. Most protest movements (1) are organized around a single issue; (2) are led by a magnetic, dedicated, and hardworking leader; (3) are unified by the fact that all of the adherents are convinced this is the most important issue of the day to them—and should be to everyone else; (4)

operate on the assumption that the initial group of members rank very high in their task orientation and have few unfilled social needs; (5) ask considerable sacrifices of their members, including time, money, skills, and energy; (6) benefit from a strong sense of social cohesion within that initial group—pluralism and diversity may come in much later in the story; (7) rally people around goals that may appear to outsiders to be vague or general, but which are perceived by those initial adherents as immediately attainable; (8) expect intense loyalty from the members; and (9) display what to the outsider appears to be a high degree of disorganization that may border on chaos and at times may result in counterproductive tactics.[1]

These generalizations can be found in the early missionary structures of American Protestantism, in the American labor movement, in new political parties, in the feminist movement of the 1970s, in most reform groups, in the ministry of figures such as John Calvin, Martin Luther, and John Wesley, in the Civil Rights Movements of the 1960s, in the populist movements of the 1880s, and in other protest movements.

The Windsor Heights Church was organized as a protest movement. As the years passed, the agenda was expanded to include several other issues including abortion, open housing, homosexuality, peace, nuclear disarmament, and hunger. Each new issue attracted some new members who were convinced that every church should place that issue at the top of the parish agenda. Several of the new issues also caused some of the original group to gradually disappear—either because they were disappointed to see the emphasis on civil rights diluted by a broadening of that issue-centered agenda or because they held a different position on that subject. Abortion and homosexuality were the two added issues that resulted in the largest losses.

The distinctive identity of this congregation as a protest movement was held together, however, by the personality, drive, commitment, leadership ability, dedication, and hard work of the founding pastor. When he retired, most of the glue disappeared.

That dynamic leader of this protest movement was followed by a minister who understood he was being asked to come and serve as the second pastor of this worshiping community. One reason he believed that was that his definition of the church was built around the Word and Sacraments. The concept of a parish as a protest movement was foreign to his theological and biblical assumptions about congregational life. A second reason is that he was in elementary school in 1965. A third reason is that he really is an introverted scholar, not an extroverted activist. A fourth reason for the mismatch was that he believed the members of the pastoral search committee when they declared, "What our people want is a pastor who will love them, who will preach solid biblical sermons, who will build a good youth program, who understands the importance of a strong Sunday school for children, and who is willing to trust the laity to carry out our issue-centered ministries."

Five of the seven members of the search

committee were completely convinced that this is what the Windsor Heights Church needed at this point in its history. Perhaps as many as a dozen of the two hundred members also believed that.

That mismatch was followed by a highly skilled reconciler and father figure who poured oil on the troubled waters and provided superb pastoral care to several troubled families during that brief intentional interim pastorate. He also believed this was primarily a worshiping community rather than a protest movement and helped move the members in that direction. The price tag, of course, was the departure of some of those original pioneers who had joined to help fulfill the goals of this protest movement.

By the time the current minister arrived, the Windsor Heights Church was well along in that transition out of the earlier role as a protest movement. The current minister came assuming this was a family-centered church and encouraged the expansion of the program to strengthen that role. One result was the appearance of more than a hundred new members who sought that type of small church. Another was the departure of many of the longtime members. A third was the conflict between the expectations of the new members and the attraction of that past role to several of the longtime members in leadership roles.

Perhaps the most significant change was from a minister who placed social justice and the creation of a protest movement at the center of his life to the current minister who had answered that question, "What do you hold to most dearly in your heart?" with the answer, "My faith in Jesus Christ as my personal Savior and my family." Those represent radically different approaches to the parish ministry!

Another influential difference is the first pastor was able to create a distinctive style of congregational life with which he was completely comfortable and which attracted only people who wanted to be part of a protest movement led by this individual.

The current minister had inherited (1) a distinctive congregational culture and tradition that had begun to erode; (2) a couple of hundred members, none of who had joined this congregation because of the attractiveness of this new pastor; (3) an uncompleted transition in role; and (4) several leaders with an agenda that did not appeal to the new minister.

What do you believe this pastor should do?

One alternative, of course, would be to resign.

A second would be to attempt to rebuild this congregation into a protest movement, but this is not compatible with the personality, values, definition of role, or priorities of this new minister.

A third would be to continue the process, already well underway, of transforming this congregation from a protest movement into a family-centered worshiping community. This new minister intuitively understands that it is easier to identify and fulfill a new role in a new setting. That, in addition to the need for a larger site, is a powerful reason to consider relocation. Four of the most useful factors in successfully carrying out a new role for any institution are (a) new leadership, (b) new goals, (c) a new setting, and (d) new players or members.

This third course of action has several implications. The first and most obvious is that the new role will appeal to a different slice of the population than the original emphasis.

Another is, a different set of organizing principles are needed to build a family-centered worshiping community than are found in a protest movement. These include: (a) placing a greater emphasis on identifying and responding to the religious needs of the members (in contrast to rallying people around a protest against the status quo); (b) recognizing the power of music; (c) expanding the ministry with children and youth; (d) giving more attention to Bible study; (e) enlarging the group life; (f) making a systematic effort to attract prospective new members; (g) devoting more time to the pastoral care of people; (h) understanding the values of organization, punctuality, schedules, agendas, delegations of authority, teacher training, and other administrative concerns; (i) affirming the legitimacy of and responding to a pluralistic agenda; and (j) lifting up a radically different approach to preaching.

A third implication is that this means a different role for the minister and requires a different set of skills.

A fourth implication that has high visibility is when a person-centered pastor follows the issue-centered minister, it is only natural to expect many of the members to be disenchanted with the new minister's goals, values, priorities, leadership style, and pastoral role. Others, who had begun to question what they believed was an excessive emphasis on issues at the neglect of people, may rejoice in this change. This can mean that longtime friends will differ sharply in evaluating the effectiveness of the new minister.

The peace of mind of the new minister also may be partially dependent on recognizing that a congregational culture developed over two decades, and one that began with a high degree of homogeneity among the original members may require considerable time to be transformed into a different approach to the parish ministry.

What do you believe are the critical variables in understanding the problems facing this new minister? Do you believe a different set of organizing principles are needed to create a family-centered worshiping community than those used by the original pastor in building a protest movement? Do you agree it is more difficult to change a twenty-five-year-old congregation than to organize a new one? These and parallel questions influence how you look at the parish ministry, and also in what you may expect of the theological seminaries.

NOTE

1. For additional insights into movements, see Kenneth I. Winston, ed., *The Principles of Social Order: Selected Essays of Lon L. Fuller* (Durham, N.C.: Duke University Press, 1981), and Lyle E. Schaller, *Getting Things Done* (Nashville: Abingdon Press, 1986), pp. 27-47. For a historical account of an urban congregation organized as an interdenominational protest movement, see Jeffrey K. Hadden and Charles F. Longino, Jr., *Gideon's Gang* (New York: Pilgrim Press, 1974).

What Do You Expect of the Seminaries?

"When I first began teaching in seminary back in the 1950s, I really enjoyed meeting with classes of men preparing for the parish ministry," recalled the professor of New Testament who had taken early retirement. "Most of them wanted to learn all they could before going out to serve as ministers of the Word and Sacraments.

"The 1960s were more difficult," he continued. "At first the problem was that while most of the people in my classes were preparing for the parish ministry, we began to see an increasing number who were still working on whether they had a genuine call from God to the ministry, and if so, whether that should be the parish ministry or something else. By the middle of the 1960s the big demand was for 'relevance,' whatever that meant. About that same time we also began to get quite a few students who were in seminary to avoid the draft. Some of them were quite open about that as their reason for coming to seminary. By the early 1970s I found myself facing six different groups of students in my introductory classes. The biggest

171

single group, but often a minority, were those preparing for the parish ministry. A second group consisted of those who were still dealing with whether or not they had a call to the professional ministry. A third group were there to avoid the draft. A fourth group consisted of those who wanted to go into some form of full-time ministry, but had zero interest in the parish. Most of these considered the local church to be an obsolete expression of the Christian faith. The fifth, and usually the smallest group, were those students who had come to seminary to decide whether or not they wanted to be Christians. Finally, each class often included one or two or three students who had a cause to advance or an ax to grind and had concluded the seminary was the best place to go to promote that cause.

"That was too much for me," concluded this widely known scholar, "and when I got the chance to take early retirement and concentrate on my research and writing, I grabbed it."

While this account does represent the reflections of a person who is now an old man—and for centuries many old men have been convinced the world is going to hell in a hand basket—it does illustrate one of the problems facing many institutions including colleges, universities, denominational headquarters, political parties, profit-making corporations, municipal governments, congregations, theological seminaries, hospitals, public schools, and newspapers.

Most institutions in our society were created for one or two purposes. General Motors Corporation was created to make money for stockholders by manufacturing automobiles. It was not created to function as an adult employment center. High schools were organized to prepare teenagers to enter the labor force or to go on to college. They were not designed to serve as retention basins for adolescents too young to take a job. Most municipal bus systems were organized to provide the public with economical and convenient transportation. They were not organized to serve as adult employment centers. The United States army and navy were created for reasons of national defense, not to prepare high school dropouts for entrance into the civilian labor force. Theological seminaries originally were chartered to prepare people to serve as parish pastors, not as a place to go to prepare to teach in a college or university. Most Protestant congregations were organized to evangelize, to gather people together for the proclamation of the Word, for the administration of the Sacraments (ordinances), and to nurture the spiritual journey of people, including children. Rarely were they organized to provide employment for the clergy.

In recent years many new responsibilities have been placed on institutions that originally were created for only one or two basic purposes. Today, for example, scores of elementary and junior high schools are expected to serve as nutrition centers, to function as surrogate parents, to provide guaranteed employment for adults, to deliver basic forms of health care, to instill discipline, to "Americanize" the children of recent immigrants, to encourage the children of recent immigrants to retain their native language and culture, to lead in the desegregation of American society, to train students to avoid involvement with street gangs, to teach birth control, to prepare students for early entrance into the labor force, to teach parenting skills to fifteen-year-old mothers, to serve as farm clubs for high school athletic teams, to provide all-day child care for the children of working parents, and to serve as neighborhood recreation centers—in addition to functioning as educational centers.

Scores of public libraries have discovered recently that parents, in search of a place to leave a child or two for a few hours because of the high cost of babysitters or child care centers, have concluded the library would be a good place to drop off their unattended child. After spending decades attempting to attract children to come to the public library, dozens of communities are now prohibiting parents from leaving unattended children at the library.

The basic generalization is the more responsibilities and obligations placed upon any institution, the greater the difficulties that institution will encounter in fulfilling what once was seen as its primary role.

This surfaced as an important issue in the creation of the new Evangelical Lutheran Church in America as policy makers debated a huge variety of expectations to be placed on parishes and on synods.

This generalization helps explain why a growing number of black parents, and especially those employed in the public schools, are enrolling their children in private schools.[1] This also is one source of the confusion about the primary role of the women's organization in several denominations. This is one of the reasons the Democratic Party has experienced difficulties in winning the office of the presidency of the United States since 1952.

This also is a source of some of the criticisms directed at theological seminaries. What do you believe is fair to expect of theological seminaries? What do you believe should be high on the list of the priorities of a seminary?

Should the top priority be preparing people for full-time service in the parish ministry? Or socializing students into the culture of that denomination? Or preparing students to serve as bivocational ministers? Or reinforcing the love of reading and learning? Or encouraging students to go on to graduate school to prepare for a career in higher education? Or to serve as an entry point for ethnic minority students into what previously was largely an Anglo denomination? Or encouraging research by the faculty to advance the frontiers of knowledge? Or to produce graduates who are expert administrators, spellbinding preachers, superb teachers, and loving pastors? Or to provide continuing education experiences for pastors? Or to train students for that growing variety of specialized ministries? Or to deepen the faith of students and assist them in their personal religious quest? Or to provide guaranteed employment for adults? Or to create centers for specialized research and study? Or to maintain a valuable piece of real estate? Or to help students find a spouse? Or to change the denominational culture and value system on divisive issues such as the role of organized labor, immigration policies, homosexuality, abortion, the ordination of women, American foreign policy, taxation, denominational mergers, support for public schools, euthanasia, public assistance for the indigent, ecumenism, nuclear power, marriage and divorce, foreign missions, disarmament, and pensions? Or should theological seminaries, like the army and navy, see themselves as institutions preparing young adults for entrance into the American labor force? Or should greater emphasis be placed on attracting and training mature second-career people for the parish ministry? Or should theological seminaries be expected to prepare students to go out as church planters immediately after graduation? Or should a greater allocation of resources be placed on the continuing education of lay leaders as part of an effort to expand the ministry of the laity? Should theological seminaries be encouraged to prepare students to go out and fit in comfortably as pastors of long-established congregations? Or should a greater emphasis be placed on encouraging students to master the skills necessary to be an intentional agent of planned change? Should the top priority be placed on preparing students to serve as *the* pastor of a smaller congregation or to serve as a program specialist on the staff of a large congregation?

That long paragraph represents only a partial listing of the expectations placed on theological seminaries today.

Do you believe those expectations are excessive? Or do you believe they are realistic?

This writer is convinced the expectations placed

on theological seminaries often are contradictory and clearly are excessive.

The most obvious reason behind this is the American conviction that education is the best solution to all problems. For example, for nearly two centuries American Protestantism has been engaged in a debate over whether or not a seminary education is necessary for service as a pastor. The evidence is mixed. Today it is clear the denominations and churches that insist on a seminary degree for ordination are somewhat less likely to experience numerical growth than those that do not have that requirement. But is a seminary degree the critical variable? Probably not. The numerical decline of what is now The United Methodist Church began about a decade following the requirement of a seminary degree for full ministerial standing, but many other factors have been more influential in that decline.

A second reason for limiting the expectations placed on theological seminaries is that only a few can be highly selective in the admission of students. Most must accept the majority of those who apply.

A third factor is the greater competition for students. An increasing number of the most committed students are bypassing the route of living on a seminary campus for three or four years and are choosing to be trained in a parish context. Many join the staff of a large congregation as lay program specialists and subsequently are ordained by that congregation. Others do that and attend school on a part-time basis as commuters while continuing as full-time staff members. The increasing number of seminary extensions or branches located on the campus of a local church make it possible to earn the degree without ever residing on the main campus of the seminary granting that degree. Others choose the twelve-to-twenty-one-month intensive "school of preaching" offered by a single congregation.

When this pattern of training the ordained staff in the context of the parish, rather than on a seminary campus, is combined with the fact that an increasing proportion of the program staff of the very large churches consists of lay specialists, it is clear why theological seminaries are having a declining impact on the culture of the very large churches.

A fourth factor has been the transformation of many theological seminaries from professional schools into graduate schools. Professional schools can be expected to train practitioners. Graduate schools are more likely to seek to prepare people to be teachers in institutions of higher education.

This conflict over expectations can be illustrated by two proposals. In one case a university-related theological seminary in the Southeast has identified its primary role as the training of scholars who will constitute the future faculty of other seminaries all across the nation. A secondary role will be to prepare other students to be practitioners. It is not difficult to predict which students will be perceived by the faculty as first class and who will be treated as second-class members of the student body.

Concurrently in a nearby state a church-related university is considering the creation of a new theological seminary that will blend a "competency based" approach to preparing students for the parish ministry with that university's academic background. The primary emphasis, however, will not be an academic approach, but rather will focus on the skills necessary to be an effective parish pastor.

This natural evolution in self-image from a professional school to that of a graduate school also produces changes in the criteria for selecting members of the faculty. Gone are the days when a majority of the faculty were ministers who had spent fifteen or twenty years as parish pastors before joining the seminary faculty. The demand today is for scholarship, not parish experience. It is difficult to find a theological seminary today in which even one-third of the faculty have spent at least seven years as the senior minister of a congregation averaging seven hundred or more at worship. By contrast, it is rare to find the surgery department in a medical school staffed by persons who have not performed hundreds of complex surgical procedures.

This contemporary emphasis on staffing theological seminaries with scholars may be one reason why an increasing number of larger churches are recruiting and training their own staff members rather than looking to the seminaries for staff. Is it reasonable today to expect theological seminaries to prepare people to serve on the program staff of that growing number of congregations averaging a thousand or more at worship?

Fifth, one of the most persuasive reasons for questioning the expectations placed on seminaries emerged from a study by two seminary professors who contend that first experience as a parish pastor may be more influential than seminary training in shaping the role and self-imposed expectations of the clergy.[2] If that first experience in the parish is a more influential formative experience than seminary, it may be unrealistic to expect seminaries to prepare people to serve as senior ministers of large congregations. This also raises a question about the ministerial placement policies of those denominations that encourage seminary graduates to begin their ministerial careers in small congregations.

A sixth factor, and one that is rarely mentioned, is a combination of two trends. The predictable trend has been that theological seminaries traditionally have been more liberal in biblical interpretation and in their theological position than the members of the churches served by graduates of those seminaries. The second trend is that, for the first time in at least a century, the United States is seeing a generation or two of young adults who are theologically more conservative than their parents. Many of the long-established theological seminaries have more in common with the generations born before 1940 than with the generations born after 1945.

One result is an increasing proportion of seminary students who are enrolled in the theologically more conservative "transdenominational" schools. Is it reasonable to expect these schools to socialize these students into the denomination in which they were reared? Probably not.

An overlapping part of that picture began to

surface in the 1970s as many people applied for admission into seminary with little or no local church background. While in high school or college they had first accepted Jesus Christ as Lord and Savior through a parachurch organization. Some were not baptized until after entering seminary. What is fair to expect of a theological seminary if its primary role is perceived as preparing these students, many of whom have never been part of a local church, for the parish ministry?

Back in the first three or four decades of this century the wide-spread assumption was that many seminary students had grown up in rural or small town America. In 1930, for example, approximately 56 percent of the American population resided in what the Bureau of the Census classified as urban communities, 24 percent lived on farms, and the other 20 percent lived off the farm in rural America.

Therefore it was not much of a culture shock for the student who had grown up in rural America to serve a small farming community congregation following graduation from seminary.

In 1988 three-quarters of all Americans lived in urban communities, 2 percent lived on the farm, and the other 23 percent were classified as rural, but that 23 percent included thousands of retirees from urban centers plus younger adults who resided in a rural setting, but commuted to an urban paycheck.

Today the vast majority of people entering seminary from a strong local church background come from large (over two hundred at worship) suburban churches. Is it reasonable to expect theological seminaries to prepare these students for their first pastorate in a small rural congregation?

Some readers may insist that the biggest single reason for tempering the expectations placed on theological seminaries is the difference in reward systems. Graduate schools usually reward the students who love books more than people, who are highly skilled in conceptualizing abstract ideas, who excel in written communication, who are strongly task-oriented, who speak when spoken to, who tend to be introverted personalties, and who display a high degree of patience.

The parish rewards ministers who are heavily person-oriented, skilled in interpersonal relationships, excel in oral communication, enjoy one-to-one relationships with people, are competent in both small and large group dynamics, who speak first, and who are gregarious, extroverted personalities, who are skilled initiating leaders, who are willing to take risks, and who are highly productive leaders.[3]

One attempt to bridge these gaps emerged many decades ago with the idea of sending seminary students out to serve as vicars or interns for a year between the middle and last year of the seminary program. This has had mixed results, partly because of the brief tenure and the lame duck role, and is now being replaced with the concept of a residency following graduation or even overlapping that last year. One pattern followed by a growing number of the very large congregations, averaging more than 1,500 at worship is to accept an intern who has completed one or two years of seminary for a one-year assignment. In fact, that really is a probationary year. If the ministerial staff and lay leadership are favorably impressed with the intern, a new agreement is proposed. Typically this calls for the intern to continue on the program staff of that congregation for the next several years. This may be a part-time relationship while the student commutes to seminary until graduation and then it becomes a full-time position. This is based on the assumption that the seminary can and will provide the desired academic preparation, but the training for the parish ministry and the socialization into that distinctive culture of the large congregation must be carried out in that parish.

What do you believe is reasonable to expect of theological seminaries? How do you see expectations changing in the years ahead? Who will initiate the most significant changes? Congregations? The seminaries? Denominational leaders?

NOTES

1. For a discussion of this recent rapid increase in black enrollment in private schools, see Lyle E. Schaller, "The Role of Private Christian Schools: Facts to Inform Your Position," *The MPL Journal*, Vol. V, 1.
2. Janet F. Fishburn and Neil Q. Hamilton, "Seminary Education Tested by Praxis," *The Christian Century*, February 1-8, 1984, pp. 108-12.
3. For a contrast between two approaches to the ministry in rural America, see Edward S. Hassinger, John S. Holik, and J. Kenneth Benson, *The Rural Church: Learning from Three Decades of Change* (Nashville: Abingdon Press, 1988), pp. 118-20.

Why Do You Want to Evaluate It?

"We're now being asked to conduct an annual evaluation of our minister," announced the person chairing the pastoral relations committee at First Church at the July meeting, "but I really don't know what we should use for criteria. Anybody have any suggestions?"

"I question whether that should be our responsibility," responded Mack Harrison, the newest member of that committee. "My understanding is we are supposed to be a support group for the pastor, a place where the minister can float a few trial balloons before going public with a new idea, and a kind of advisory group. I have great difficulty with this idea that we should evaluate the minister's performance. That could create an adversary relationship between our committee and our minister. Our job is to support the minister, not to determine whether our pastor should be commended for doing an excellent job or should be reprimanded or dismissed. Let the finance committee make that evaluation before it brings in a recommendation on next year's salary.

If they won't do it, maybe it would be better to appoint a special ad hoc evaluation committee. Our role is not to judge the pastor's performance but to encourage, support, assist, and advise the minister."

* * *

"According to this report from our evangelism committee, only 23 percent of all our first-time visitors eventually unite with our church," commented Sarah Brown who had been studying the annual reports submitted by the various committees and board. "I think we need an evaluation of our whole new-member enlistment system to see what the problem is. That 23 percent figure seems awfully low to me. We need to identify what the barriers are and remove them."

* * *

"When we adopted this new schedule with two worship services and Sunday school in the middle, we agreed we would wait eighteen months before evaluating it," recalled Fred Radcliffe, a member of the board at Trinity Church. "It's now two years later, and I think the time has come for an evaluation of the schedule. I don't know about the rest of you, but I'm still hearing complaints from people who prefer the old schedule."

* * *

These three calls for evaluation appear on the surface to raise the same issue. In each case the request is for an appraisal of a particular subject. A closer examination, however, reveals they represent four different approaches to evaluation.

Mack Harrison's response to the suggestion that the pastoral relations committee should conduct an annual evaluation of the minister clearly was based on a definition of the word *evaluation* as meaning to judge or grade. That has long been a common and widely used operational definition of the term. The teacher evaluates the student performance by giving a grade. The boss evaluates the work of a subordinate by rewards, reprimands, bonuses, and other actions that may include a promotion or dismissal.

A sharply different, and more recent definition of *evaluation* was used by Sarah Brown when she questioned that 23 percent figure. Sarah was convinced that more than one-fourth of all first-time visitors eventually should unite with that congregation. She had made a judgment on the performance. She saw it as substandard and unacceptable. Sarah's call for an evaluation was a request for information that would improve the new-member enlistment process. That is a different definition than Mack Harrison was using for the word *evaluation*.

The request for an evaluation of the change in the Sunday morning schedule represented two other definitions of the term. It appears that Fred Radcliffe's request for an evaluation was motivated by the hope this would supply a response to the critics of the new schedule. That is a remarkably common motivation for seeking an evaluation. While one facet of such requests is to secure a judgment, either good or bad, the primary reason for seeking an evaluation is to silence the critics. A variation of this is the attempt by many committees to pass the buck by deciding to "appoint a committee to study it and bring in an evaluation." Sometimes that represents an effort to buy time in the hope the critics will either disappear or pursue a different issue.

A better quality reason for a request for an evaluation of that new schedule would have been based on a fourth definition of that term. Such an evaluation would have been designed to reveal the congruence between the goals and the actual outcome. Ideally, these goals would have been stated and quantified in advance. That list of goals might have included these eight measurable items.

1. To increase the proportion of members who attend worship at least three to four Sundays in the typical month from the present 43 percent to at least 60 percent.

2. To increase the number of members who attend worship at least twice in the typical month from the present 320 to at least 450.

3. To increase the number of members attending at least once a month from the present 425 to at least 500.

4. To increase the total attendance on the average Sunday from 335 to at least 500.

5. To increase the average attendance among the adult Sunday school classes from 165 to at least 250.

6. To at least double the number of first-time visitors each Sunday morning by (a) reducing the crowded conditions at the eleven o'clock service and (b) offering people a choice of time when they could attend.

7. To double the number of greeters and ushers each week.

8. To spark the creation of a new adult choir for the early service with an average attendance of at least eighteen with no decrease in the size or the choir at the second service.

If these eight goals had been formulated before changing the schedule, and if the statistical benchmarks had been established, it would have been relatively easy to determine whether or not the performance matched those earlier expectations.

A far easier, but less useful form of evaluation would have been to go back to the judgment format. This might have been as simple as passing out a short ballot on an average Sunday and asking all those present to check one of these two statements:

1. Do you favor retaining the new schedule?
2. Do you favor returning to the old schedule of Sunday school at 9:30 A.M. followed by worship at 11:00 A.M.?

This second approach would have provided the policy makers with a measurement of the degree of dissatisfaction or satisfaction among the members with the new schedule. It would not have enabled them to measure the impact on participation.

If the policy makers had wanted only to evaluate the feeling level of the members, it might have been useful to use a somewhat more complex question. One form of such a question could resemble the following instrument.

On a scale of −10 to +10 we would like to discover your response to the new schedule. Please write a number in this space _____. If you write a +10, you are expressing the highest possible degree of satisfaction with the new schedule. A +9 would represent a slightly lower degree of satisfaction. A +5 would be moderate support. A zero would represent complete neutrality—you really don't care one way or another. A −10 represents the highest possible degree of dissatisfaction with the new schedule. A −5 represents a moderate degree of unhappiness with the schedule. You may use any number between −10 and +10 to express your response.

The eight-question format illustrates the use of evaluation to measure performance against expectations. The two-question ballot represents an evaluation effort to determine support for the new schedule versus a return to the old schedule. This last scale can be used as an evaluation tool to measure the depth of support for change versus the degree of opposition to change.

If the primary purpose of the evaluation was to elicit suggestions, ideas, and comments to improve the new schedule, the procedure might be designed to ask for those kinds of reactions, suggestions, and recommendations. In other words, the primary purpose for carrying out an evaluation should influence the design of the evaluation effort.

Six Questions

As you reflect on using evaluation procedures in your congregation, consider these questions.

1. What is the *primary* purpose for a particular

evaluation effort? To produce a judgment? To gather information for use in decision making? To test the congruence between expectations and subsequent performance? To be able to respond to critics of change?

2. Does the design of the evaluation tool and the process match that primary purpose? Will it provide the data you seek?

3. Are you more concerned with quantifying the differences in opinions or with measuring the depth of people's feelings on this subject?

4. If you have more than one need to be met by this evaluation effort, will the questions and instruments you use meet all those needs?

5. If you are seeking data to inform the decision-making process, do you have some means of giving more weight to certain responses or do you plan to give equal weight to every response?

For example, how do you weigh the responses from (a) the member who rarely attended before and now only rarely attends but happens to be present when you pass out those evaluation sheets; (b) the member who rarely attended before but now rarely misses that early service; (c) the person who was a regular attender before and still is a regular attender, but for personal reasons refuses to unite with your congregation; and (d) the member who rarely is absent?

Will you poll only those persons who are present on a particular Sunday? Or will you poll the entire membership? Will you poll the occasional visitor and the first-time visitor? If so, will you give the same weight to every response? Will you give zero weight to an incomplete questionnaire?

6. How do you plan to inform the members who participated in this evaluation process of (a) what was learned from that effort and (b) what the impact will be on policies, program, staffing, finances, and schedule?

One of the common sources of discontent among church members is to participate in an evaluation effort, but never learn the results and/or the impact of that evaluation.

Three Reservations

When you think about evaluating a program, schedule, staff member, or activity in your congregation, keep these reservations in mind.

The first is evaluation can create adversary relationships, enhance alienation, and undercut morale. This, of course, is a greater danger whenever the evaluation process is designed to render judgments, to grade performance, or to discontinue certain programs or activities. This is a risk whenever the evaluation process is designed to produce winners and losers.

Second, if the evaluation is to be used to measure performance against expectations, it is essential these expectations be clearly articulated *in advance* and that widespread agreement be reached on the ranking of the critical expectations. Thus, if this approach is to be used to evaluate the performance of a staff member, it is vitally important that the staff member know in advance what these expectations are, that they be quantified in measurable terms whenever possible, and that agreement be reached on what constitutes the four or five most important expectations including agreement on which expectation is at the top of that priority list.

Likewise it is useful to formulate in advance the criteria for subsequent evaluation whenever a new program is launched or when the schedule is changed or when a new staff position is created or when a building program is planned.

Finally, it usually is somewhere between unfair and excessively optimistic to expect any standing committee to evaluate its own performance. Likewise it may create dysfunctional conflict in role to expect the mutual support committee for a staff member (such as the pastoral relations committee or the Christian education committee) to evaluate the performance of that staff member.

As a general rule it may be more practical to appoint a special ad hoc committee to conduct the evaluations of both program and/or staff. In each case, however, it is extremely important for the special committee to understand the primary reason behind that request for evaluation. Is it to make a judgment on whether or not to continue that program (or staff position)? Or is the primary purpose to inform the decision-making process? Or is it to answer the critics? Or is it to measure the congruence between earlier expectations and subsequent performance?

The clearer that definition of the primary purpose, the easier it will be to devise the appropriate process and questions.

What do you believe is the primary purpose behind the evaluation procedures used in your congregation?